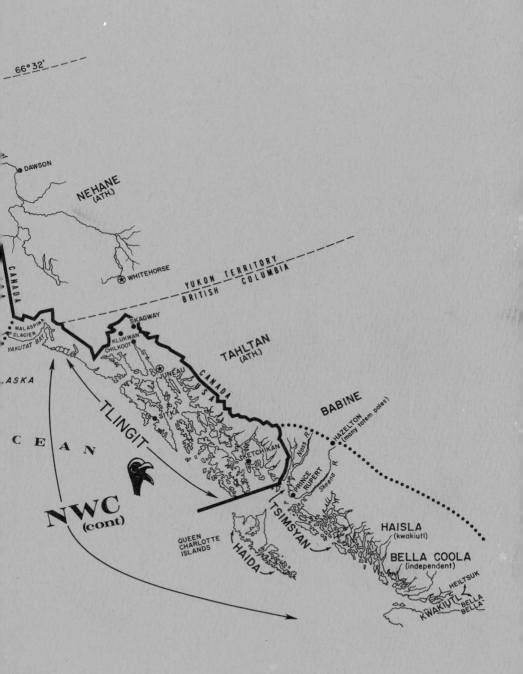

66° 32'

DAWSON

NEHANE
(ATH.)

CANADA

WHITEHORSE

YUKON TERRITORY
BRITISH COLUMBIA

MALASPINA
GLACIER
YAKUTAT BAY

SKAGWAY

KLUKWAN
CHILKOOT

TAHLTAN
(ATH.)

ALASKA

JUNEAU

CANADA
U S A

TLINGIT

SITKA

BABINE

HAZELTON
(many totem poles)

KETCHIKAN

Nass R.

O C E A N

NWC
(cont)

Skeena R.

PRINCE
RUPERT

HAISLA
(kwakiutl)

QUEEN
CHARLOTTE
ISLANDS

TSIMSYAN

BELLA COOLA
(independent)

HAIDA

HEILTSUK

KWAKIUTL

BELLA
BELLA

Other Books by Joseph H. Wherry

Economy Car Blitz

The MG Story

The Jaguar Story

The Alfa Romeo Story

Automobiles of the World

Famous Firsts in Automobiles

The Totem Pole Indians

Indians of the Golden State (in preparation)

Indian Masks and Myths
of the West

INDIAN MASKS AND MYTHS OF THE WEST

JOSEPH H. WHERRY

Funk & Wagnalls ❧ New York

FH

FOR

my Paiute friend Michael Rogers,
his Yurok wife, Alta,
their daughter, Pauline,
and all American Indians who seek
to preserve their magnificent heritage

Acknowledgments

THE AUTHOR wishes gratefully to acknowledge the generous assistance rendered by Mr. and Mrs. Sidney Parish of the Tsunúnu Shinal band of the Pomo; Mrs. Dale McCarty for her skillful handling of photographic negatives, some of which were exposed under rather difficult conditions; Mr. Wayne Colwell of the California Department of Parks and Recreation; and my wife, Bettye, for her indispensable typing and editorial assistance.

Special thanks is also due the many institutions whose directors have graciously permitted the author to photograph artifacts from their collections. Initials designating each institution owning the artifacts concerned are included in the explanatory captions accompanying the illustrations. The institutions are:

RLMA   The Robert H. Lowie Museum of Anthropology, University of California, Berkeley

AMNH   The American Museum of Natural History, New York City

MAI   Museum of The American Indian, Heye Foundation, New York City

USNM   United States National Museum, Smithsonian Institution, Washington, D. C.

NMC   National Museum of Canada, Ottawa
PMBC   Provincial Museum of British Columbia, Victoria
MPM   Milwaukee Public Museum, Milwaukee
PM   Peabody Museum, Salem
CNHM   Chicago Natural History Museum, Chicago
UMUP   University Museum, University of Pennsylvania, Philadelphia
CSIM   California State Indian Museum, Sacramento
OPM   Oakland Public Museum, Oakland
PAM   Portland Art Museum, Portland, Oregon
WCHM   Willis Carey Historical Museum, Cashmere, Washington
MPA   The Museum of Primitive Art, New York City
DAM   The Denver Art Museum, Denver, Colorado
TM   The Taylor Museum, Colorado Springs, Colorado
UMDA   University of Minnesota, Department of Anthropology, Minneapolis

Grateful acknowledgment is also directed to those community and state organizations and institutions which have supplied photographs from their files; these are credited with the author's thanks.

Preface

SCRATCH a modern American Indian and you still find a human being who is metaphysically a part of the spiritual universe in a way that is incomprehensible to most Americans of European descent. Not only are the world view and language of the modern Indian an indispensable part of his psyche if he is to maintain the dignity of his race, but an appreciation of these psychological necessities by his fellow Americans is just as necessary to their own well-being.

An illustration of the extent of the carelessness with which the Republic's governmental structure treats the Indian occurred early last year. Several public officials including a prominent senator were "investigating conditions" on the pitifully sterile forty-acre rancheria of a band of the Pomo in northern California. After a speech to the Indians and their white neighbors, the prominent senator asked one of his companions "How do you say 'good-bye' in Indian?"

The instinctive politeness of their race prevented sharp retorts from the Indians within hearing, but the condescension of the senator was not lost on them. The senator did not understand that a Pomo, for example, is as distinctly a nationality—in comparison to an Apache or a Nez Perce—as is an Irishman, a Dane, or a Roumanian.

Indians who have been raised with knowledge of their ancient ways have a unique and admirable code of ethics and morality that makes them one with nature and nature's God. Perhaps this is why some of the ancient ceremonies are still practiced despite several hundred years of external legal restrictions. This is why the ancient masks are used in a few places where the myths still have meaning and provide a frame of reference that makes the world and the universe tolerable in a materialistic and cynical age. The Indian's god, "The Great Oversoul," is still through all and in all. Traditional myths are a part of the ancient faiths, and masks illustrate the supernatural powers. Precise photographic reproductions of the sacred masks of some tribes are taboo; other tribes have no such restrictions. We have sought to abide by the tribal tenets. Not all Indians of the West had masks, but all had a vital mythology. Where there were no masks, we have employed photographs of other cultural artifacts.

Our *original* Americans possess a rich heritage, but they have been betrayed on every hand for nearly half a millenium.

In *The Totem Pole Indians*, published in 1964, the author appealed for the establishment of a national American Indian Day. Senator Warren G. Magnuson of Washington and Representative Don Clausen of California introduced resolutions in the Senate and the House for such recognition, but to no avail. Despite days and weeks promoting everything from newspapers, milk, and better bread to clean roadsides, the American Indian has yet to achieve recognition; he still struggles for survival in a land he once possessed from sea to shining sea. We have much to learn from our Indian brothers and sisters, and the greatest lesson is tolerance.

Contents

Indian Masks and Myths

of the West

1

The People and the Far West Culture Regions

Lo, the poor Indian! Whose untutor'd mind
Sees God in clouds, or hears him in the wind.
—ALEXANDER POPE (1688–1744),
Essay on Man

ontrary to the bigoted hypocrisy of Cotton Mather, who urged his fanatical followers to slaughter "those pernicious creatures," and the bloodthirsty notion advanced by General Sheridan at Fort Cobb in Indian Territory—"The only good Indians I ever saw were dead"—the race we call American Indians had well-developed and satisfying philosophies that enabled them to live in harmony with nature. This alone was no mean accomplishment. By comparison, twentieth-century "civilized man" appears determined to assure his own destruction by tampering with and seeking to improve upon nature.

3

One of the Southwest's great prehistoric ruins is in the Wupatki National Monument some 30 miles north of Flagstaff, Arizona. The ruined houses indicate a substantially stable culture and suggest that the inhabitants included ancestors of at least some of the present Pueblo tribes. Flagstaff Chamber of Commerce

The aboriginal Americans had come to terms with their surroundings long before Europeans arrived on the scene. In the vanguard of the latter were those who vigorously preached the doctrines of a dozen sects that promised the original Americans a better way of life. Because this way of life was invariably accompanied by force and total conquest, prohibiting the free practice of aboriginal religion, it is small wonder that to this day the Indians' acceptance of the new faith has been largely of the lip-service variety.

To understand the American Indians—specifically those of the Far West—it is necessary to examine the traditions by which they lived. Having no written language—the usual means by which we gain knowledge of a people—the Indians are at a disadvantage through no fault of their own. Their conversational manners evolved around a refusal to interrupt a speaker until he had had his say, but the European rarely accorded the conquered the same consideration. Consequently the expanding Europeans seldom allowed themselves the privilege of learning precisely what the Indians believed. Even today representatives of the Great White Father rarely listen with open minds. Remarkably well-kept journals of European families long resident upon this continent (including those of the author's ancestors) usually record one-sided details of contact with the native inhabitants, rarely recording what the natives had to say in their own behalf. There were too many Mathers and Sheridans, too few like Bartolomé de Las Casas, an American-born Spanish priest of the sixteenth century who pleaded unsuccessfully with the crown of Spain and the church hierarchy for humane treatment of the natives. Protestants did no better, but as with their Catholic counterparts, there were isolated and brief localized instances of enlightenment.

Prejudice, hypocrisy, and greed outweighed any desire to learn the details of the Indian faiths, the primitive roots of which came with the first arrivals out of Asia. Archaeologists have found evidence of migrations into and across central Alaska during the late Pleistocene era. This places man in the New World at the same time as the extinct camel and horse, the mammoth, the giant beaver, and the giant bear. The latter undoubtedly inspired some of the myths of the Northwest Coast. The discovery in 1965 of a human skull

5

scientifically dated as between eleven thousand and thirteen
thousand years old (reported to the press on April 30, 1968,
by Senator Warren G. Magnuson) places man near the junction of the Palouse and Snake rivers in southeastern Washington at an earlier date than had been considered previously.
Other human artifacts, like eighty-five-hundred-year-old
vegetable-fiber footwear in eastern Oregon confirm fairly
widespread early wandering throughout the Plateau Region.
Other discoveries point to man's migration southward through
our subject area into Mexico around thirty thousand years
ago.

Clothed in the mists of time beyond the knowledge of Indians at the time of discovery, the ancient colonizers of North
America brought with them the primitive traditions of the
lands of their origin. Successive migrations crossed the land-
bridge between Siberia and Alaska and quite likely traveled a
later sea route, skirting the Aleutian Islands, which could account for the "out of the foam" tradition. All of these movements account for the wide diversity of physical types represented by the natives of the continent and our subject area.
The endpaper map with the linguistic and tribal key gives
reason to the variety of myth forms and the investigative
problems experienced by physical and cultural anthropologists.

Some of the ancient myths have evolved through thousands of years. The best of these are related herewith; they
provide the best means for understanding the traditions by
which the Far West Indians lived. The Indians revered their
traditions above all material possessions, for they provided

*Related to the famed Yaqui tribe in the
State of Sonora are the Mayo, who use
masks like these in the Pascola dances. Of
the Cahita division of the Piman family,
the Mayo are thus linguistically related to
the Pima and Papago tribes of Arizona.*
RLMA by Joseph H. Wherry

6

their link with the infinite. Indian children grew up with these myths and were secure in the knowledge that they were the creations of the Great Oversoul and of a spiritual universe that could not be rationalized to three visible dimensions. The individual's soul blended indivisibly with that Great Oversoul which permeated and was a part of everything animate and inanimate. Interdependence between man and man and between man and every aspect of nature was more than an idealistic theory—it was a way of life held together by the web of tradition.

But how many of the traditions are myths? How many are legends with some basis in fact? No one can say with any degree of certainty, and this adds to the charm of Indian mythology. A *legend* is a story combining historical fact with tradition; while a *myth* is usually defined as a predominantly religious story based upon supernatural or unknown origins. Note that neither definition implies lack of some truth. Consequently myths, being mainly of a religious nature, are clothed within a mysterious framework. The mythological traditions of a people interpret real or imagined history and provide legitimacy and understanding to an existing state of affairs and environment.

Anthropologists recognize four basic types of myths, the characteristics of which often blend together. The beginnings of the deities or supernatural beings are contained in *theogonic* myths; whereas *culture* myths relate how human or animal-like supernatural beings instructed man in various crafts and ways of life. Imaginary occurrences believed to be responsible for certain customs or social organizations (such as clans and tribes) are the subject matter of myths classified as *etiological;* while *nature* myths supply an interpretation of the origin and functions of the earth, the elements, and the universe. The various myths related in the following chapters include all of these types.

The more developed the native culture, the more complex was the mythological framework—the equivalent of a literary tradition—that enabled the Indian to understand his world. We find, therefore, the myth patterns of the Southwest and the Northwest Coast were the most sophisticated in the Far West. A relatively easy way of life in the California region allowed the leisure time for a fairly extensive mythology in contrast to that of the Plateau and Great Basin regions. Sustaining life in the latter region was extremely difficult, and the myths, consequently, were quite simple in content. An examination of the several environments and ways of life clarifies the relative simplicity or sophistication of the mythological traditions.

The Southwest Culture Region

All of Arizona, New Mexico except for a small northeastern triangle included in the Plains culture (not a part of our subject), and a small strip of California west of the lower Colorado River comprise the Southwest region. Close to eighty thousand Navajo on the largest reservation in the United States—larger than Connecticut, Massachusetts, Rhode Island, and Vermont combined—dominate the scene in the northern part of this region. Of Athabaskan linguistic stock, the Navajo and the Apache tribes are related. While the Navajo can be considered a single tribe with many clans, the Apache include several tribes with the best-known historic divisions being the Chiracahua (of the great chief Cochise, the prophet-medicine man Geronimo and Victorio) the Coyotero, the Lipan, the Arivaipa, and the Jicarilla, generally on the west side of the upper Rio Grande. East of that

9

The remarkable Cliff Palace in Mesa Verde National Park inside Ute country in southwestern Colorado. Ancestors of several of the present Southwest tribes, the inhabitants built sturdy rock houses and hunted wild game on the mesa above. The round structures were kivas, ceremonial chambers similar to those of many present Pueblo tribes. State of Colorado

great river in New Mexico the Mescalero Apache and other Lipan bands roamed; while farther northeast the Kiowa-Apache, though linguistically related, were confederated with the Aztec-Tanoan-speaking Kiowa of the Plains in and beyond that corner of New Mexico, not truly a part of the Southwest culture region.

Nomadic hunters and warriors, the Apache and their Navajo relatives are comparative newcomers within the past one thousand years. To the early Spanish conquerors

Apaches de Navajo was the term that distinguished the Navajo, who roamed and raided over northern Arizona and the northwest part of New Mexico, from the Apache tribes. The latter also moved about the entire Southwest region. Together and separately, these warrior-nomads made life miserable for the older settlers, the Pueblo Indians, the Pima, the Papago, and the Colorado River tribes. Eventually the Navajo began to trade with the stable Pueblo tribes, from whom they learned agricultural skills. When the Spanish introduced sheep and horses, the Navajo became skilled herdsmen, and both of these large, virile tribal groups used the horse to increase their military talents and their areas of influence.

Longer in the region, the Hopi are of Aztec-Tanoan linguistic stock; they now occupy seven villages—*pueblos*—on three mesas near Keams Canyon where their reservation, completely surrounded by modern Navajoland, approximates the lands they occupied when the warlike Navajo and Apache arrived. Other related Aztec-Tanoan-speaking peoples plus others speaking Keresan dialects of the far-flung Hokan-Siouan stock occupy a score of ancient pueblos on the upper Rio Grande and west as far as Zuni. Skilled dry farmers and most jealous of their ancient heritage, the pueblo-dwellers have managed to maintain an admirable purity of race and a culture that has changed little since Coronado invaded the seven old Zuni villages in search of the fabled Seven Cities of Cibola in 1540.

This vast, seemingly inhospitable area was the homeland of other tribes, too, when the first Europeans arrived. Long before the Christian era, however, Folsom and pre-Folsom men lived in caves and hunted animals before climatic conditions changed as the last glaciers retreated farther in the North. After Folsom men came the Hohokam Basket Makers, who probably learned pottery-making from Mexican tribes to the South. These ancients devised stone, stick, and mud houses around and over pits. Invaders from the North and West arrived about fifteen hundred years ago, and possibly some speaking Aztec dialects came from the South; ancestors of the Pueblo people of today, they eventually built magnificent pueblos. Greatest of these was Pueblo Bonito in Chaco Canyon, a huge apartment-type city housing at least twelve hundred people according to archaeologists. Of the existing pueblos, the most famous is Taos north of Santa Fe.

Over near the Arizona border the very conservative Zuni claim the ancient pueblo-builders as their ancestors, as do the other tribes in Puebloland. The world view of the Zuni is quite typical of all the Pueblo people; in fact there are similarities with the cosmogony related in the Navajo creation myth in a later chapter. Zuni tradition holds that their ancestors emerged from the underworld to the earth's surface and searched for their "center," where they would have water and security. Coming to the "White House," where traditions of many Pueblos say the people learned about their gods—Yellow Woman, for instance, who was chief of the Corn Maidens—the priests were led by Water Spider to "the place of the ants." Astride an anthill, Water Spider touched the horizon in each of the four directions, proclaimed the place where he sat to be the center of the world, and instructed the people to build their village at that location. The only organized town in Zuniland is Halona, which means "ant hill" to this day. Significantly, most aboriginal Indians "knew" their place of living to be the center of the world or the universe.

The spiritual pantheon of the Pueblo Indians is composed of beneficent rain gods, hunting gods, and other deities—*kachinas*—who were created when the "first people" came to the earth's surface. These deities reside in the high mountains surrounding the pueblos. Nearby are the flat mesas and valleys where the fertile but dry soil has been tilled for more

Indians of several tribes living on the Warm Springs Reservation in Oregon, Plateau country, still fish for salmon in the Deschutes and other tributaries of the Columbia River as their ancestors did, with spear and net. Now the "forever" years of their treaty rights are numbered. The associated Warm Springs tribes now own and operate unique but modern wilderness camping grounds complete with a tipi motel. Note the geological rift line in the background. Oregon State Highway Dept.

than a thousand years. When the Spanish came, they found these Indians raising their colored corn (maize), beans, and varieties of squash. In the circular temples—*kivas*—the priests and the men of the Snake, Antelope, and other sacred societies conducted the ceremonies to invoke the kachinas who brought the rain and good crops and aided in the hunt. The famous kachina dolls, miniature representations of the

13

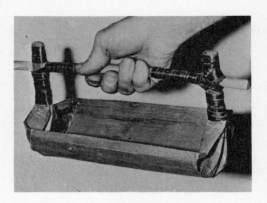

*Simple, quickly made carrying baskets suf-
ficed to contain small objects in village life
during the winter months when deep snow
covered the Plateau region. The tribal origin is not recorded, but the basket is not
ancient.* WCHM by Joseph H. Wherry

deities, are presented to children during ceremonies as a necessary part of their instruction in the mysteries of life. (The
heads of the kachinas best illustrate the ceremonial masks of
the Pueblo tribes for, not being holy in themselves, they can
be illustrated. Masks worn by the dancers are holy; hence it
is a violation of sacred taboos to illustrate them with photographic reproductions. The author is aware that photos of
the masks of the Pueblo Indians have appeared; when this
occurs, either the reproduction is unauthorized or the masks
illustrated have been prepared especially for the purpose. In-
considerate violations of sacred taboos—whether intentional
or through ignorance—are but additional instances of failure
to observe proper deportment when dealing with our original
Americans.)

Though possessing less wealth than the Pueblo Indians,
and consequently, a simpler mythological tradition, the related Pima and Papago Indians lived anciently in that portion of the Sonora Desert which extends north of the present

14

Mexican border toward Phoenix. In ancient times there were some dwellings similar to those of the Pueblo region scattered about this desert area, but for a thousand years or more these speakers of other Aztec-Tanoan dialects have constructed no adobe or masonry multiple-family dwellings. Instead they have used cactus rods and such desert vegetation as they could scrounge to build flat-topped dwellings that often were plastered with adobe. Often the floors were excavated a foot or two below the surrounding ground surface. Ingenious farmers, the Pima dug irrigation canals through which they brought the life-giving waters of the Gila and Salt rivers to their parched land where they raised corn, squash, and cotton. The other major Piman tribe, the Papago, live today on the lands of their ancestors, probably the most difficult land in the United States for farming. The low-lying desert of Papagoland is starkly beautiful with the stately saguaro cactus. Seeds, berries, and edible cactus supplemented their corn, which seldom reached more than two feet in height; while rabbits, a few birds, and antelope rewarded hunting parties with occasional meat.

The gods of the Pima and Papago were those of nature, and shamans derived their power from visions and dreams. Tribalism did not exist among these hardy desert dwellers; the clans were loosely organized around villages that rarely consisted of more than a dozen separate family houses. Skilled basket- and pottery-makers, like most of the Southwest's Indians, the Pima and Papago were essentially village-dwellers and farmers.

Constant raiding by the everpresent Apache tribes, however, found the Pima and Papago quite able to defend themselves with bows and arrows, spears, and war clubs. Frequently these desert-dwellers took the warpath in retaliation, even in comparatively recent times. During a Pima raid in 1871 on a band of marauding Apache, the Pima captured a

15

One hundred years ago Chief Moses—Half Sun—of the Sinkiuse in eastern Washington was as well known as Chief Joseph of the Nez Perce. Warrior Chief and statesman, he was also a respected medicine man. Today his descendants live on the Colville Indian Reservation in northeastern Washington with a dozen other once great Plateau tribes. Wenatchee Daily World

Some tribes are striving to renew the old traditions, and modern versions of the ancient tribal "schools" function in a few places on the West Coast. Here, in a brush house—an unroofed circle of green branches—two Pomo youths assist a little fellow in his initiatory public appearance in the Feather Dance at night by firelight. Joseph H. Wherry

five-year-old boy, Wasajah, whom they sold to a prospector named Carlos Gentile. Because the prehistoric Casa Montezuma—an impressive five-story cliff dwelling of unknown origin and now a National Monument—was in Pima territory, Gentile gave the boy the surname of Montezuma. For a first name the boy took Carlos after his owner. Gentile was good to his little Apache, took him to Chicago and put him in school. To make a long and poignant story short, Carlos Montezuma eventually graduated from the Chicago Medical College in 1889 and immediately became a doctor with the Indian Service. After serving his red brothers, the Western Shoshoni in Nevada and the Plateau-region tribes in Colville, Washington, Dr. Montezuma taught in the College of Physicians and Surgeons in Chicago. From 1897 on, this Apache doctor carried the plight of his Indian brothers to the public through lectures and writing, a career that might never have materialized had the Pima not captured him during a raid on his own people.

It is believed that the Pima and their Papago relatives may have acquired a few masks in pre-Columbian or early historic times from their relatives the Yaqui. The latter tribe was of the Cahita division of the Piman stock and occupied the area between the Gulf of California and the Sierra Madre in Sonora, from whence bands of them occasionally roamed into what is now southwestern Arizona. Incidentally, the Yaqui like many tribes in the United States, have no treaty—they have never formally submitted to the government of Mexico.

Scattered along the Colorado River from its mouth in the Gulf of California all the way to the Grand Canyon were the Yuman tribes which spoke various Hokan-Siouan dialects. Ethnologists customarily divide them by their traditional geographic territories along the river as Upland or Lower Yumans, the latter ranging below the big bend of the Colorado or south of present-day Lake Mead. Southernmost was

17

the Cocopa tribe, which lived just above the river mouth and seldom ventured north of modern Yuma city on the Mexican border where their lands adjoined those of the Yuma (proper) tribe. The Mojave were the largest and fiercest of these desert-dwellers; they dominated the lower two hundred miles of the river's course. Least warlike was the Maricopa tribe, which though related, was constantly on the defensive. In early historic times the Maricopa moved eastward into Pima and Papago country. Although granted reservation status, neither the Maricopa nor the Mojave have a treaty with the American government. In general these lower Yumans tended toward the Arizona side of the Colorado—with the exception of the Mojave, who claimed considerable land in the desert that now bears their name. All were good farmers and raised corn, squash, pumpkins, and melons in the fertile bottomlands, but without irrigation. Mesquite beans, seeds, piñon nuts from the forests, antelope, deer, and birds were also eaten. Not canoe-builders, these Indians used rafts and reed balsas when they crossed the river. Garish body paint and tattooing were tribal customs. Clans existed but were rarely named, and their flat-topped brush and thatched-roof square houses were scattered, with villages few and widely spaced. An unusual mortuary custom among aboriginal Americans was cremation of the dead.

The three upland Yuman tribes were the Walapai, the Havasupai (prehistoric offshoots), and the Yavapai. The latter were the only Yumans who scorned tilling the soil. Ranging from the river's big bend toward the center of modern Arizona where they hunted extensively, the Yavapai were confused with the Apache by settlers as were the lower-river tribes who were called "Mojave Apache" by the whites until fairly recent times. Best known of the Upland Yumans were the Havasupai—"people of the blue water" in their own tongue—who have lived for centuries in one of North Amer-

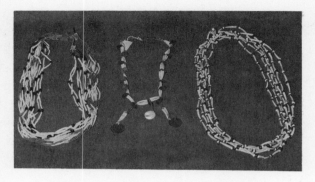

Strings of the tusk-shaped dentalium shells were the most valued medium of exchange among the California and Northwest Coast tribes. The Plateau tribes obtained dentalium in trade, too, mostly through the Chinook of the lower Columbia River and the Coast Salish west of the Cascades. The Nootka and Kwakiutl became wealthy because their tidal lands contained the most easily obtained dentalium. CSIM by Joseph H. Wherry

ica's most beautiful and isolated valleys near a waterfall close by the west end of Grand Canyon. Their adobe and brush houses resemble Navajo hogans. Even today when they have embraced telephones, radios, and other modern conveniences they prefer these dwellings. Havasupais irrigate their fields much as did their ancestors who habitually climbed to the forested plateaus in the autumn to gather pine nuts and to hunt the abundant game. Havasu Lake above Parker Dam on the Colorado River is named for them.

In general the southern parts of Arizona and New Mexico are desert lands and lack snow during the winter. The opposite condition prevails over much of the northern half of both states where elevations vary from three thousand to seven thousand feet with numerous higher peaks intermingled with the Painted Desert in Navajoland and other summer deserts. Winter snows and many streams, canyons, and variegated

19

topography and vast forests provided the Pueblo, Navajo and Apache peoples with a lovely land which they adapted to a happy way of life under circumstances that many modern Americans find difficult. Other Indians of the Far West were less fortunate.

The Great Basin Region

Scorching in summer and cold in winter for the most part, the Great Basin lies between the Sierra Nevada on the west and the Rocky Mountains on the east. Most of Idaho, the southwest corner of Montana, the western halves of Wyoming and Colorado, all of Utah and Nevada, the southeast part of Oregon, and a slice of California make up this vast region. Sustaining life here was more difficult than anywhere else in North America, with the possible exceptions of the Piman country south of Phoenix and the bleak habitat of the Eskimo on the continent's fringe. Except for the Washo—or the eastern slopes of the Sierras around, north, and south of Lake Tahoe—who spoke a Hokan-Siouan dialect, all of the Basin tribes were linguistically related. Seed- and piñon-nut gatherers, the Washo lived like many of the California Indians.

The area was a wasteland with large alkaline areas and only scattered springs and waterholes; sagebrush, mesquite and runty cacti were the predominant vegetation. Coyotes, a few kit foxes, groundhogs, gophers and similar rodents, mountain lions, and bear on the higher ground around the Basin provided occasional food. Hunting jackrabbits, deer and antelope that were driven into box canyons or brush nets was a tiring enterprise before the arrival of horses in historic

20

Yurok young ladies proudly wearing their ceremonial garments of bleached buckskins decorated with olivella shells and dangling rectangles of haliotis. The maiden in the middle wears extremely valuable multiple loops of dentalium shells around her neck. In June, 1965, a dozen Yuroks displayed signs quietly to bring attention to the treaty signed four generations ago by their ancestors. The U. S. Senate still has not ratified that solemn treaty. Joseph H. Wherry

times. Throwing sticks much like boomerangs and other crooked sticks enabled fast hunters to kill fleeing rabbits on the run or to extricate them from their holes. To the horror of early whites, some Basin tribes ate snakes, field mice, and grasshoppers when the supply of grass and wild grain seeds dwindled. Nor was the Indians' liking for the tasty chuckwalla, a fat lizard that grows to around eighteen inches, an understandable appetite. Scantily clothed in rabbit and coyote skins or with kilt-like garments made from grasses, the region's Indians cultivated no crops simply because condi-

21

tions rarely permitted such activity except in the Chemehuevi-Shoshoni territory adjacent to the Yuman tribes.

Because they dug with pointed sticks for tiny wild potatoes and other nutritious roots, whites called the natives "diggers" and subjected them to derision and physical indignities. Staying alive took all the skill a person could muster against a harsh environment. Dwellings of rocks or brush wikiups around pits scooped out as insulation against summer heat and freezing winters added to the legends of the "diggers" one hears to this day from unlearned Anglo-Saxons who still laugh at the way "Grandpa used the Indians in his mine as cheap labor for a few scraps of garbage."

Dominant throughout this region were Shoshonean tribes speaking Uto-Aztecan dialects of the more extensive Aztec-Tanoan linguistic stock. Shoshoni tribes, some known as Paiute, ranged across much of Nevada and into Southern California where they, too, had merged into the California culture when Europeans arrived. The related Gosiute held a territory west of the great Salt Lake in Utah; while some of the Ute enjoyed a better life with more plentiful game in the Uinta Mountains of northeastern Utah, a range a bit out of the ordinary geologically, as it lay from east to west (most mountain ranges lie in a north-south direction). The Wind River country of Wyoming and the southwestern part of that state were northern Shoshoni territory; in fact, this division of the widespread tribes had a culture similar to that of the Plains Indians.

Sacagawea, who guided Lewis and Clark on their epic

The warlike tribes of the far Northwest Coast often used helmets and armor in battle. Said to be very old, this Tlingit wooden helmet is decorated with hair, and there are traces of red and black paint. The tough moose-hide body armor is painted with the stylized symbols of Bear. RLMA by Joseph H. Wherry

1804–05 exploration to the mouth of the Columbia River was a Shoshoni. Captured years before by Hidatsa-Sioux, the "Bird Woman" was the purchased wife of the French Canadian trapper Toussaint Charbonneau, whose own principal contribution to the expedition was to overturn a large canoe. Plunging into the icy waters of the upper Missouri River, Sacagawea rescued the parfleche containing all of the valuable exploration records. Without Sacagawea, Lewis and Clark would not have been able to obtain horses, nor could they have crossed the Continental Divide. The guardians of the Divide where they crossed were a Northern Shoshoni band led by Bird Woman's brother.

Due to the terrain, the various Shoshoni-related tribal groups moved about considerably, but within fairly well-defined areas. Southernmost of the Basin Shoshoni were the Chemehuevi on the western side of the upper Colorado River; northernmost were the Bannock and Lemhi of eastern Oregon and southern Idaho. Distantly related through linguistics were the Hopi of the Southwest and the warlike, buffalo-hunting Comanche of the southern plains, a region outside the scope of this volume.

Despite the vicissitudes of life the Basin Shoshoni proved to be sturdy adversaries in battle. As recently as February, 1915, hostiles of the Weeminuche band on the Ute Reservation in southwestern Colorado made medicine with some of their Navajo neighbors across the state line near Four Corners and, after a pitched battle with a large force of U.S. marshals, came close to full-scale warfare with the cavalry. The story of this last Indian outbreak is well told in Forbes Parkhill's *The Last of the Indian Wars* (The Crowell-Collier Publishing Company, 1961). Some of North America's finest basketry is still made by many of the Shoshoni and the Washo, and all of them were skilled makers of spears, clubs, and bows and arrows. When horses came to

Like a mask but nearly three feet long is this Kwakiutl potlatch-feast-bowl cover, an indication of the quantity of delicacies set before a chief's guests at such important gatherings. MPM by Joseph H. Wherry

the Basin, all braves who could obtain mounts became excellent horsemen. Some of the Wyoming Shoshoni followed the buffalo, and more than one well-defended wagon train and military outpost felt the sting of Shoshoni, Ute, and Paiute raiders seeking to defend their sacred lands. On the northwest flank of the Basin, the so-called Snake Shoshoni were frequently at war with the Cayuse of Oregon.

Ceremonies were few in this region, and the mythology was of the campfire variety, as later chapters will reveal. A Paiute friend believes that a few dancing masks were used "in the old days," but the author has been unable to trace any. This region produced another phenomenon, the Ghost Dance, which upset the West and precipitated the last Sioux War of 1890–01, which ended when defenseless old men, women, and children were slaughtered by troops equipped with repeating rifles and Hotchkiss rapid-fire field pieces in a massacre called "The Battle of Wounded Knee" by a War

Department as competently led as was the 7th Cavalry regiment in 1876. Before the latter date the northeastern Shoshoni tribes had reached a military status on par with the Plains nations. Fortunately for the westward-moving whites, the great Shoshoni Chief Washakie (Shoots the Buffalo Running) liked the pioneers and befriended hundreds of them as they struggled through the passes across the Divide in Wyoming. Sadly the whites have not reciprocated, for scheming speculators are still conniving to oust the descendants of Washakie from their Pyramid Lake holdings and the few other fractions of ancestral lands the Basin tribes have managed to retain.

The High Plateau Region

Moving out of the Basin brings us to the area drained by the Snake and Salmon rivers, the southeastern part of the Plateau region where the Cayuse, great horse-breeders, held the northwestern Shoshoni Snake tribe at bay. Animals and birds were plentiful in eastern Oregon, Washington, the panhandle of Idaho, northwestern Montana, and parts of two Canadian provinces. Arriving early in the eighteenth century, the horse gave increased mobility to a score or more of tribes which previously had their villages in river valleys. Salmon, sturgeon, and other fish as staples were supplemented with nourishing camas roots and a vast variety of wild grains and berries. There was no need to engage in farming. Hot summers were more bearable than in the Basin because of year-round rivers and streams, forested hills, and prairies between the Cascade Mountains and the Rockies. Heavy snowfalls were, and are, common during winter

One thin piece of straight-grained red cedar was bent, carved, and painted by the Nootka to make forehead Wolf masks like this. If the wearer wished to hide his identity, he covered his face with strands of shredded cedar bark. As a guardian spirit, Wolf bestows happiness and hunting success. NMC by Joseph H. Wherry

months, and snowshoes were used whenever these secure Indians ventured outside their lodges.

The dominant tribes were of the Shahaptian linguistic family of the same Penutian stock as the Tsimsyan of British Columbia and the Chinookian tribes of the lower Columbian River. Covered later, the Chinook were middlemen in the lively trading of shells and other coastal products, particularly the esteemed dentalium, tusklike shells that passed through the middle Plateau country to the westernmost Plains tribes in eastern Montana. Straddling the trade routes were the Nez Perce, so called by French-Canadian *voyageurs* because their nose septa were pierced to hold a dentalium ornament. This custom was not as widespread as some accounts have implied.

Although great hunters, the Nez Perce had well established villages with small and large permanent houses, the latter holding up to four dozen families by the late prehistoric

27

period. Wood crafts included canoes throughout the region. Most tribes had hereditary chiefs, and clan organization was usually lacking. Their enemies on the east, the Piegan and Crow, were not always able to prevent these vigorous people from forcing their way across the Continental Divide for an occasional buffalo hunt. The Umatilla of Oregon, the closer Walla Walla, the wide-ranging Yakima nation, and the Klickitat had a similar hunting-fishing culture. All of these tribes became excellent horse Indians, as the regimental journals of several cavalry and infantry outfits attest. In the mid-nineteenth century the Yakima and their allies in central Washington campaigned against the encroaching settlers. By 1876 a series of broken promises and treaties forced even the peaceful, largely Christianized Nez Perce under Chief Joseph into the running war of 1877, which pitted less than two hundred warriors against several regiments and elicited the admiration of General Howard and Colonel Nelson A. Miles after months of fighting through the Rockies. The Nez Perce were trying to reach the sanctuary of Canadian soil.

In the southern part of the region were the related Klamath and Modoc tribes, neither of which had embraced the new horse culture to any great extent. Again pressure forced these Indians, particularly the Modocs, to a final defense under Kintpuash ("Captain Jack" to the whites), which led to a classic stand with only about seventy warriors in the lava beds near Tule Lake in northeastern California in 1872–73. Outnumbered six to one and more by regulars, a battery of artillery, and volunteers under General E. R. S. Canby (who

From a grave house on Admiralty Island, this Tlingit mask symbolizes a dying warrior. Shamans used such masks to illustrate their gifts as restorers of life and vitality. Ceremonies telling of battles also required such realistic masks, for the Tlingit were a warrior race. AMNH by Joseph H. Wherry

29

lost his life in this war), the unmounted Modocs proved their mettle but eventually went down to defeat.

In the northeast of the region were the Algonkian-speaking Kalispel, often called the Pend d'Oreille, and the so-called Flathead Indians of the Idaho panhandle and western Montana. Forehead-flattening of infants during their cradle months was widely practiced throughout the northwest by the Salish tribes of the Algonkian linguistic stock. Medical research in the late years of the last century disclosed *no* physical or mental impairments from this custom. Just above the "Big Bend" of the Columbia River in Washington the other Salish tribes—all related to the Coast Salish covered later—were dominated by the Okanogan, a powerful tribe with territory on both sides of the present international boundary; the Methow were nearby and allied. These became horse warriors, too, and by 1800 were becoming as much like the Plains tribes as were the Nez Perce, Yakima, and Umatilla.

Farther north were the Kootenai, the Lillooet and other tribes of the Fraser River area in British Columbia, and the Nicola-Ntlakyapamuk and Chilcotin. The latter two were of Athabaskan stock, distant relatives of the Apache and Navajo far to the south. Throughout the Plateau region life was good, and dreams and visions provided the basis for less formal religious practices. Thus the mythology was simpler than that of the Southwest and of the two regions remaining. Basket- and weapon-making was a serious business, but there was no pottery. Clothing was of skins, with antelope, deer, some elk, plenty of rabbits, bear, and mountain lions providing the hides and furs. Meat, of course, was in abundance and included mountain sheep and goats for those tribes near the high Cascades and upper Rockies. Eagle-feather headdresses were preferred to masks, but the leather mocca-

30

This mask from the Queen Charlotte Islands was made by an unknown Haida. The
almost black coloring suggests it was used
either in a funeral ceremony or to represent an unknown Negro sailor on one of
the countless trading ships that dropped
anchor in Haidaland from c.1800 onward.
NMC by Joseph H. Wherry

sins, leggings, and the like were of comparable quality to those elsewhere on the continent.

The California Region—Indian Paradise

California was paradise for a kaleidoscope of tribes and bands speaking dialects of four large linguistic stocks plus several other dialectic groups—at least until Europeans arrived. What the Spanish began, the Americans finished with genocidal barbarities and bounty hunting that decimated the Indians.

According to the Bureau of American Ethnology, there were probably around 150,000 Indians in what is now California when first contacted by the Spanish in the fifteenth century. At least 100,000 Indians remained, although a number of distinct tribes had disappeared, when California was annexed by the Union in 1846. By 1876, just thirty years later, barely more than 20,000 full-blooded natives remained. Early records describe the savagery of the "militia" units organized to hunt down the native people. One account relates how an early settler, in a humane moment, used a small-caliber gun on children because the big bore 45–70 rifle slugs "tore them up so much." Equally revolting is the stupidity of Federal authorities who paid out around $900,000 for the expenses of the "volunteers" and bounty hunters who took it upon themselves to slaughter the "diggers," as the good settlers and miners called them, in the 1850s and 1860s. The purchase of Indians for servitude was common less than a hundred years ago, especially of orphaned Indian children. When he editorialized in the local newspaper against a white massacre of Indians in the Humboldt Bay area, the famed

An unusual mask said to represent Lynx, this was found in the first Christian church in old Metlakatla, Alaska. Allegedly Tsimsyan, this could be a Tlingit mask, possibly representing the indigenous and valuable Sea Lion—a powerful guardian spirit who inspired wealth. PMBC by Joseph H. Wherry

Brett Harte had to flee Eureka to save his own skin. Finally, to add insult to injury, the U. S. Senate never got around to ratifying a batch of solemn treaties the California Indians had signed in good faith. The "Eighteen Lost Treaties," as the California Indians still call them, remain at the core of the problems the natives of the Golden State seek to remedy now.

As indicated by the endpaper map, tribes of Shoshonean stock were most numerous in southern California. In ancient as well as recent prehistoric times there must have been considerable trade from the coast across the Mojave and Colorado deserts. This would account for the prevalence of abalone shells among the Southwest region's tribes and for the tradition of "Changing Woman" or "Turquoise Goddess," the Navajo deity whose "home" is on an island in the sea off the West Coast. The Chumash, a Hokan-Siouan speaking tribe living along the coast in the Santa Barbara area, built excellent planked, seagoing canoes and developed a prosperous culture based upon fishing and hunting. In the Central Valley and in the mountains bordering it, the Yokut, Maidu, Patwin, and Wintun tribes and their neighbors spoke Penutian dialects. Their culture included village life and seed-, nut-, and acorn-gathering. Acorns pounded into a meal and leached to remove the tannic acid were an important staple all over California, and nowhere was farming seriously practiced. Northward along the coast the Salinan and Pomo were important groups speaking Hokan-Siouan dialects; the latter were and are the finest basket-makers in the Americas. Pomo feathered baskets are jewel-like works of art without peer.

The coastal area drained by the Klamath and Trinity rivers comes under the Northwest Coast culture region, but inland in northern California the Miwok, of Penutian stock (who also held the present Marin County coast and carried on friendly trade with Sir Francis Drake during his extended visit in 1579), held territory in proximity to the Hokan-Siouan Yuki, Wappo, and Shasta and the Athabaskan Mattole, Sinkyonne and Wailaki. By no means is this a complete list of the California tribes, which still provide ethnologists with much scope for scholarly research; a more complete list of tribes with their proper linguistic affiliations accompanies the map.

Curiously only the Chumash, already mentioned, made large wood canoes. Lake- and river-dwelling Indians con-

34

structed balsas of reeds, some of them remarkably like those still made by the Indians around Lake Titicaca in Bolivia. Dwellings were often brush structures similar to the wicki-ups in the Southwest, while the Miwok, Pomo, and others often used bark strips for their lodges and round ceremonial dance houses. The latter were traditionally covered with soil and are reminiscent of the Southwest kivas but for the entry-way facing the east instead of the roof entry in the case of the Pueblo tribes.

If there was anything wrong with the climate and food supply in most of the California region, it was that both flora and fauna were in such abundance that tribal organization and discipline was rare. Most of the tribes found living so easy that they had become unaccustomed to vigorous de-fense. Hence, the appearance of aggressive Spanish, Mexi-cans, and Americans overwhelmed them too easily. Warfare had become a formalized, almost ritual-like contest among most tribes. When serious military adventures were under-taken, the war parties were relatively small, and long cam-paigns over a wide area were virtually unknown after the his-toric period began. Moreover, the absence of true military societies or organizations within tribal bodies and the lack of alliances between tribes for either defensive or offensive pur-poses obviated any widespread effort to resist Europeans. The native Californians were simply too good natured for their own welfare, as matters developed; their aboriginal Golden Rule was never reciprocated. Consequently, the only two fairly sizable reservations the Indians managed to retain, Round Valley and the Hupa-Yurok lands in the northwest, are being hacked away as this is written—the "Lost Trea-ties"—and the former will be destroyed completely if present government plans to build dams are implemented. Nowhere in the West have Indian affairs been so grossly mismanaged as in California, although the broken treaties regarding fishing rights "in perpetuity" in Washington state run a disgracefully close parallel. Remarkably the tribes have kept some of the old traditions and ceremonies alive and a few native religious activities still relate to their ancient beliefs, as will be observed in a later chapter.

Northwest Coast Region

This region begins about two hundred miles north of the Golden Gate. On the west side of the Cascade Mountains, this narrow strip extends all the way to Yakutat Bay in southeast Alaska. From the latter southward to Gray's Harbor in Washington, the area detailed in the author's book *The Totem Pole Indians*, the culture developed around the totemism described in the last chapter.

Athabaskan-speaking Tlingit and Haida nations, the latter Queen Charlotte Island-dwellers in the main, came under strong Russian influence early in the eighteenth century. Spanish and English explorers also had visited them by this time. Warlike, the northerners were excellent craftsmen. Large seagoing canoes, carved from a single huge cedar log, enabled them to engage in trade and raiding southward as far as Vancouver Island, which was held by Kwakiutl and Nootka tribes of the same linguistic background. The Olympic Peninsula of Washington, the southwest coast of British Columbia, and the area surrounding Puget Sound were Coast Salish territory. The numerous tribes and bands were ethnically related to many of those of the Plateau region east of the Cascades, but their way of life was far different.

Chinook tribes spoke Penutian dialects similar to the faraway Tsimsyan and occupied both sides of the lower Colum-

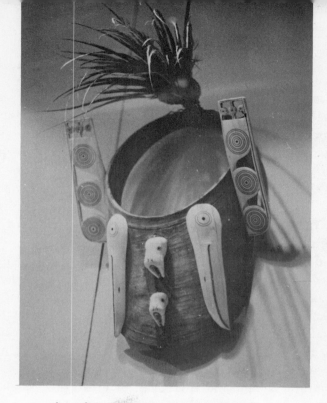

A traditional design, this Aleut "hat" or sunshield, collected before 1898 by the Alaska Commercial Company, displays symbols of supernatural birds, possibly suggesting Fulmar. The two small carvings could represent Walrus. Aleut masks are rare and often realistically show human faces. RLMA by Joseph H. Wherry

bia river, where they did a lively trade in slaves. Raids by the Northerners along the lush coasts of Washington and Oregon and, according to tradition, as far south as northwestern California enabled the Chinook to become prosperous middlemen by selling the captives to the upriver tribes and even to the westernmost Plateau tribes. By the same means the tusklike dentalium shells, gathered from the sea bottom along Vancouver Island shores and elsewhere in the far Northwest, found their way to the interior where strings of them were the equivalent of the wampum of the Eastern Indians. Oregon coastal tribes were of Penutian and Athabas-

37

kan stock for the most part. Depredations by early settlers virtually destroyed the tribes along the Rogue River and its tributaries, particularly the Chetko, who lost a large village of more than forty houses and some three hundred people in 1853.

Well-established villages with adz-cut rough-plank houses stood along river and sea shores "in the old days." Row upon row, the houses on Vancouver Island and northward were decorated inside with short totem poles—house posts—while outside totem poles of forty feet and higher were elegantly carved with family or clan crests and stylized representations of guardian spirits. Totem poles contained the carved symbols of real or mythological events of importance in the life of the owner or in the history of his ancestors. In the ceremonies, all of which had a strong religious foundation, masks were worn, and these too were carved with the figures of supernatural beings and mythological creatures. Early missionaries often assumed that the totem poles and masks were venerated, that the figures on the poles were images and objects of worship. Hence hundreds of such works of native art were destroyed by Indians who were convinced by ill-informed missionaries that they would surely suffer the fires of hell should they continue carving totem poles or permit the existing ones to stand. Countless dancing and ceremonial masks suffered the same fate. Fortunately, however, many have been preserved after being acquired by knowledgeable persons. Many of these are shown here, without violating tribal taboos, and explained in the accompanying captions. Nowhere else in all of North America were there masks of such great variety and interest. Only in the Southwest were ceremonial masks as important.

South of Puget Sound totemism and guardian spirits decreased in importance, and the carving of totem poles and masks gave way to headdresses of feathers, sea lion tusks,

This flat-nose Eskimo mask from the Anvik area on the lower Yukon River represents a woman with chin-tatoo marks. The hair is green, and it appears that there was originally a top piece of baleen. The carver either lacked skill or did not complete this mask. University of Alaska Museum

and fur, and headbands and streamers of feathers. Smaller canoes were of the short dugout variety, whereas those of the Northern tribes often carried upwards of thirty people complete with all of the equipment necessary to wage war or to set up temporary camps away from their permanent villages. Baskets were woven throughout the region.

Everywhere salmon was the staff of life. Berries, wild lettuce, or onions, and the meat of bear, mountain goats, deer, and rabbits supplemented the succulent fish and other seafood delicacies such as halibut, oysters, clams, lobsters, and crabs. Sturgeon were also plentiful in the region's rivers. Among some tribes, clan taboos eliminated bear from the

Made of whalebone and 10 inches long, this bizarre figure was made by an Eskimo at Point Hope. This could be a rare variant of the half-face masks shown elsewhere. Dinah E. Wólf, Curator of Ethnology at the University of Alaska Museum, states that this mask is "made to be hung on the wall—not to be worn. The eye is ivory with a baleen pupil. Made in 1967 by a man who said that his mother was born with one eye and 'the shaman cured her and gave her two eyes.' I have never seen one like this before, although whalebone masks have been made at Point Hope for many years." University of Alaska Museum

menu. Seal- and deerskins were used in the manufacture of clothing, as was shredded cedar bark. In the north, ermine pelts were used to decorate the garments of chiefs, and mountain-goat wool was made into garments.

Class distinctions were the most elaborately drawn of anywhere on the continent. Of top rank were the aristocracy, to whom the accumulation of wealth and its ostentatious display was essential to the maintenance of status and reputation. The supreme gathering of the clans in the North was the potlatch given by a wealthy chief. The more gifts the chief gave to his guests, who came on invitation, the more obligated were the guests to reciprocate. Often, to prove affluence—and to reëstablish influence—a chief would order the destruction of valuable possessions such as blankets or "coppers" or canoes. On occasion slaves would be given away, sold, or clubbed instantly to death as further evidence of great wealth—an aboriginal equivalent of lighting a cigar with a five-dollar bill or giving away large sums to favorite charities with prearranged publicity. Of descending status were commoners and slaves; the latter were often well treated. Society was generally matrilineal in organization.

Mild throughout most of the region for most of the year, cold weather persisted only for a few winter months. Snow fell only in the extreme northern part of the region, and rain forests abounded with game animals and birds. Dense redwood forests extended into the southern part of Oregon; northward fir and red cedar prevailed. From these durable and insect-resistant woods, large family and clan houses were built before Europeans arrived; a few still survive in isolated areas away from the haunts of vandals who delight in destroying ancient artifacts. In recent years Indians of the Northwest Coast have begun to reëxamine the traditions of their ancestors. The result is a renewal of some of the old crafts by scattered Indians. Without doubt the interest of museums and anthropologists has inspired tribal leaders to conserve their heritage.

The Region Beyond

Beyond Yakutat Bay the coastlands of Alaska are the habitat of the Eskimauan family. The island-dwelling Aleuts are a branch of this large linguistic stock which spreads across the top of the world from the neighboring Yuit of Siberia to Labrador and the frozen wastelands of Greenland. *Aliuit* was the name applied to islanders from the Diomedes through the Aleutian chain by the early Russians whose occupation decimated the Aleuts. Here as elsewhere throughout North America, however, the natives call themselves by various names which in their own dialects almost always mean "the people."

Fishing and hunting provided the way of life and still does for most of the natives. Dense forests supplied the wood for dwellings in the Aleut and Eskimo villages. Carvers made delicate spirit masks decorated with whale baleen and feathers. Walrus-tusk ivory and whale and seal bones are also crafted, as are the hides. Conical wood hats were also popular among the Unalaskan and Atkan divisions of the Aleut, and fine basketry of grasses and roots was regionally made. Physically the Aleuts differ considerably from the neighboring Eskimos, the Inuit, who are medium in height, stocky of build, and very strong. By contrast, the Aleut tend to be taller and more slender. Social organization is informal, and a village council governs the local community under a head man who is usually elected. There are no chiefs in the hereditary or monarchial sense. Dreams, visions, and a belief in spirits is the basis of the native religion.

Inland Alaska is inhabited by Athabaskan Indians, the Khotana, the Ahtena, and the Talhtan tribes from about 160 degrees West and 65 degrees North, longitude and latitude respectively, eastward and southward to territories adjoining the Tlingit and Tsimsyan nations of the Northwest Coast. Generally nomadic, except for periods between hunting expeditions when they stayed close to their scattered villages on the tundra, the interior Indians were influenced by the Eskimo and the aforementioned Indians. Other than dogs, the caribou was the most important animal on the interior.

Horses never became a factor in the cultures of California, the Northwest Coast or the Arctic West. All travel was by foot, canoe, dog team, or skin boat, the latter in the far North. Religious faith was the cement which brought reality and understanding to all of the native peoples of the Far West, and when immediate disavowal of ancient traditions was demanded by the Europeans, the social fabric came apart, creating a disarray that has never been repaired. The great dignity of all of these people is most admirable.

Creation and the
Beginning of Light

he place of the beginning is somewhere in the universe, but precisely where is not always clear.

This tradition of a period of darkness and chaos reminds one of the evident time lapse between the first and second verses of Genesis, which is basic to the Judeo-Christian doctrine of conscious beginnings.

The Navajo Creation

The great Navajo nation's doctrine of the dawn of the present age chronicles the adventures of the first three living beings, Coyote, who was a creator and trickster, First Man, and First Woman. Groping about their cramped first world in complete darkness, the three decided to journey to the second world, where there was a faint yellow light in the West,

44

a glimmer of white light in the North, and a dim blue light in the South. The East, from whence they had come, was black, and there was a living being in each direction. The travelers found two people in the second world, Sun Man and Moon Man, and they observed that the three colors glowed brightly and it was day. At other times the black from the East blanketed everything and it was night. During the first day Sun Man forced his affections on First Woman, but she resisted and an argument broke out. To settle matters, all-knowing Coyote cried out, "Beings in the four directions, come here for a council so we can determine what to do; this second world is too crowded."

The beings came and everybody sat down on the ground after the proper ceremonies. Soon all present agreed with Coyote that more space was needed.

"Come," said Coyote, "let us all climb the sky ladder to the third world."

After a long, arduous climb they stepped out onto a spacious expanse of land with trees, mountains, canyons, lakes, rivers, and beauty everywhere. The People of the Mountains met Coyote and his followers.

"We are happy to welcome you," said the Mountain People, "and everything will go well here with you as long as the water monster is not disturbed."

Coyote, always thinking of tricks, considered the warning. "I'm going to search for the water monster," he mumbled as he started toward the East where the big waters were. Finding the water monster's home and the water monster's two children, Coyote liked them so well that he put his blanket around the children and carried them away to his own home. When the water monster Tieholtsoti returned to his home and discovered his children were missing, he thrashed about in a rage and went off to search all over the world for them.

"My children have been stolen," Tieholtsoti said to him-

A quintet of lovely Apache princesses in their treasured tribal finery during a recent annual Inter-Tribal Pow Wow in Flagstaff, Arizona. Flagstaff Chamber of Commerce

self, "so I will use my power on the waters and cover the land."

Swiftly the low places became oceans and the oceans rose and flooded over the land and the Mountain People, after a short council, took the mountains from the four directions and piled them all together. All the people now climbed to the top of the new mountain where they planted a fast-growing hollow reed which soon grew through the sky above the third world and into the fourth world. Up through the reed all of the people and their animals climbed. Bringing up the rear was Turkey, who began to climb when the flood waters reached his tail feathers. To this day all of Turkey's descendants have white-tipped tail feathers, proving that their ancestor had to flee the flood.

After four days and nights of climbing, the people stepped out onto the fourth world, which was very dim. The murky light seemed to come from three sources, but the land and mountains and lakes were much like those of the former world. The broad land was divided from East to West by a wide river. Human people lived on the North side, while the South side was populated by animal people. The situation seemed idyllic, but a year was as short as a day and a controversy arose between men and women because time passed too quickly.

"We are most important," said the men, "because we build the houses and hunt for food."

"You are wrong," the women countered, "because we bear the children, plant and harvest corn and cotton, make all of the pottery, and even build the fires and keep them burning."

"Ah," the men replied, "but we know the proper ceremonies and dances which keep the spirits happy. We certainly are more important than you because our ceremonies assure good crops. You could not live without us men."

When the quarrel worsened, the men made a large canoe and crossed the river to the South side where they built houses, planted crops, hunted animals for their meat, and had more food than they could eat. Meanwhile, on the North side of the great river the women planted no corn or cotton, and after four years they were sad. The men were sad, too, and at a council of the sexes they all decided that each needed the other and each was as important as the other. So the families were reunited after confessing the argument had been ridiculous.

They resumed the responsibilities for which each was fitted and this is how men and women learned to live together peaceably as families. Expanding their farming activities,

A Navajo brass band: the Navajo nation knows it lives in the twentieth century. The second gentleman from the right wears the emblem of a well-known railroad which has its own Chief. Flagstaff Chamber of Commerce

the people spread across the land and their families grew and new families were started. Everything was fine, or should have been but for one thing. Old Coyote was living quietly in his house, and he still held the water monster's charming children captive because of his fascination for them. Unaware of the evil in their midst, the people were so happy that they were unprepared for the tragedy about to overtake them. At first the moisture in the ground was not noticed, but when the great river overflowed, the wise men said, "We must hasten and prepare for another flood!"

Once again the people struggled to move the mountains together from each of the four directions. In the middle of their cultivated land they piled the mountains together into one and climbed to the top where they planted a hollow reed as their ancestors had done so long ago. Quickly the reed grew through the sky above the fourth world.

"Badger, you must lead the way," the wise men ordered, "because you have sharp claws and can dig through the sky."

So Badger went up first through the giant hollow reed, and it was good that he did because the sky over the fourth world proved to be dirt. As Badger dug, the earth-sky became muddy, and presently all of the people emerged from the reed to discover they were in a vast sea of mud.

"What shall we do?" the people wailed. "The flood is still rising and will engulf us and we will drown."

"I can get through the mud," Locust volunteered. "I will find the way to dry land." And he scrambled through the mud, half-flying, and went up to the surface where he saw a yellow swan in the West, a blue swan in the South, a white swan in the North and a black swan in the East like the lights in the previous worlds. After listening to Locust's account of the trouble all of the people were having getting away from the flood the swans proclaimed everyone would have to pass a test in order to enter the fifth world.

"Everyone must thrust an arrow into his mouth and down through his body and pass it completely through," the swans said. "Then the arrow must be reversed and drawn up through each person's body and be brought out through the mouth," they said as they demonstrated how easily this was done.

Locust knew he could do this bit of magic but he also knew the people could not. "I'll agree if you will do as I do," said the crafty Locust, who drove the arrow through the middle of his body—or appeared to do so—and withdrew it from his backside. Locust's magic was that his spine was very short and did not extend the length of his body; thus he was able to pass the arrow through his body below his spine.

"Now let me see you do what I have just done," Locust challenged.

"We agree that your magic is as powerful as ours," the swans replied. "Summon all your people to enter."

Up came the people in great haste, each man, woman, and

child carrying his small bundle of treasured possessions. Out into the great muddy swamp they climbed, but the flood waters rose behind them and there was no dry land.

"There is the water monster," called out one of the people in a loud voice. "There is Tieholtsoti. I see his horns above the mud!"

Sure enough, the terrible water monster was there. "Come over here, all of you," Tieholtsoti commanded. "Let me see all of your belongings. Unwrap your bundles!"

The people had no other choice, and Coyote, who was among them of course, had to unwrap his blanket.

"Coyote has Tieholtsoti's children," the people murmured. "Coyote, that old trickster, is the cause of all of our troubles!"

The water monster was happy to see his beloved children and the people pushed them to Tieholtsoti without delay. The waters receded rapidly as the reunited water monster family swam away, but the people found themselves standing huddled together on a large island in the center of the swampy sea.

Now the priests ordered them to be quiet while they prayed to the black god of darkness in the East. Immediately the god cut through the mountains and the waters flowed through the canyon.

"But there is still too much mud," the people complained. "We still must stand here huddled together."

Next the priests had the people pray to the winds of the four directions, and a great wind blew for four days until the mud was dry.

"Now we can go to the land," the people rejoiced, and they did so, but because the ground was not correctly shaped the wise men and chiefs put them to work moving great masses of the remaining mud. On each of the four corners of the new fifth world they made mountains which quickly hardened. The entire world grew and the mountains grew. Instructed

by the wise men and priests, the people grabbed hold of Sun Man and threw him into the sky. They also threw Moon Man into the sky. Every day for four days the world grew and the Sun rose higher into the sky until, on the fifth day, the Sun of the fifth world was at its highest point but it stood still.

"Now it is so hot everything will be burned as quickly as it grows," the people protested.

"We must have a sacrifice for the Sun," a wise man decreed and the wife of one of the high chiefs was prepared as an offering. When the last breath and drop of blood had left her body, the Sun began again to move in his orbit.

"This is a sign," said a wise man, "that people will die as they grow old. Do not be afraid, for this is as it should be." And the priest walked to the place where the people had emerged and looked down through the great hollow reed. "I see our chief's wife," the priest told the people. "She is happy and healthy and is beside the great river in our old world."

The priest looked down again and listened to the woman who had just died. Turning to the people, the priest said,

"Our chief's wife told me that everyone in this new world will return to the old fourth world after they die and there they will live in great happiness forever."

Sun moved across the sky from East to West every day. During the dark of night, Moon was supreme. One day the old priest died and Coyote—who knew everything—told the people that this meant that a Navajo would die every day and that during the night someone also would die. From Coyote's interpretation of these events, the people came to believe that anyone who looked upon a dead person would die and this— the Navajo creation story—tells us why the face of a dead person is covered quickly with a blanket and the body is buried so the spirit can emerge into the other world of eternal happiness.

Later we will see how the various tribes came to be. First, though, a visit to Shoshoni country in the Great Basin is in order.

Shoshoni Law and The Milky Way

When the aggressor in a fight loses, he is banished forever from his tribal lands. This Shoshoni law is responsible for the creation of the trail of stars in the sky. It happened this way.

One day Wakini the black bear was feasting in an anthill he had found. Suddenly without warning Wakinu the grizzly, who had come down from the Sierra, ambled up and without so much as a greeting tried to get in on the feast.

The annual Pendleton Round-Up in September brings the chiefs and bands of Bannock, Snake, Nez Perce, Shoshoni, and other Plateau tribes together for one of America's greatest native pow wows. Tribal elders usually establish a traditional tipi town, and Indian mounts, Cayuses and Appaloosas, are raced and traded. Plains-type regalia with porcupine-quill breast-plates were common on the Plateau by 1800, but the modern drum is out of place. Oregon State Highway Dept.

"I found this anthill," Wakini growled. "This is mine and you have no right to it."

"Then I'll take what I want whether you like it or not," Wakinu snarled as he lashed out at Wakini with his long, curved claws.

"No you won't," retorted Wakini, and the fight was on.

No doubt the knowledge that he was in the wrong contributed to the defeat of the mighty grizzly. Similarly, knowing that he was right enabled Wakini to fight harder and with greater skill, because he gave Wakinu a sound and thorough thrashing.

A Coast Salish youth of the Lummi tribe near Bellingham, Washington, on Puget Sound, where the culture was similar to that of the vigorous Kwakiutls. Washington State Department of Commerce and Economic Development

"Now Wakinu," the chief of the bears said, "you must leave this land forever. Go now!"

Hanging his head in shame, Wakinu the grizzly shuffled away with tears in his eyes as he realized he would never see his tribe or his homeland again. On and on he traveled, hardly noticing where he was going, until he came to a high place where it was freezing cold and dark. Snow covered the ground as far as he could see, but the only sound which came to Wakinu's ears was the whistle of the wind and his own feet crunching on the snow. Wakinu had climbed so high that he was above timberline. He wondered what he would eat and he feared he would starve to death. In the distance

54

where the black sky touched the ground Wakinu could see a faint glow.

"I'll run and see what that glow is," Wakinu thought, and he ran so fast that his feet seemed to be flying.

"I am flying," he shouted. "I really am flying." And Wakinu, the disgraced grizzly, was flying. Up into the air toward the glow rose Wakinu, and as he rose he shook the snow from his silver-tipped fur coat.

Far away in the camp of the black bear and grizzly bear tribes, his former friends and tribesmen were watching the sky. What they saw made them stare in wonder.

Wakini, the victor in the terrible battle, stared the hardest. "Do we see a big bear flying up into the sky?" his tribesmen asked Wakini.

"Yes," replied Wakini, "that is Wakinu. He has found the way to the Heavenly Hunting Ground."

"But what is the silvery trail behind him?" said the other black bears. "Tell us, Wise One."

"Wakinu is shaking the snow crystals off his silver-tipped coat as he rises into the sky," Wakini answered. "The white crystals will always be there in the sky on clear nights to light the way to the Land of the Souls. The trail of stars is the Bridge of the Souls. In the future all people will call it the Milky Way."

Farther to the Northwest in the redwood forests the ages of Creation are also in progress. Here, too, Coyote is a creator when he is not playing tricks. In the lands of the Pomo, the Yuki, the Miwok, the Hupa, the Karok, and other nations including the Yokuts east of the Coast Range, Coyote was faced with an awesome task.

Coyote Makes People in California

A great flood plus gigantic earth fires had destroyed the first people, including Eagle, who was the wicked earth ruler. Finally Coyote decided that conditions were again suitable for new people. So Coyote called a council of his best friends. There was Frog Woman, who was Coyote's wife; Kingfisher, who ruled the sky; and Lizard, who was excep-

Danger threatened when Thunderbird made thunder by flapping his wings. When lightning flashed, the monster bird was shooting arrows at the earth. When his wings relaxed, all was peaceful. These conditions were illustrated on the great totem poles of the far Northwest Coast. An unknown Bella Coola made this Thunderbird or Eagle mask of wood, then covered the beak with eagle skin. NMC by Joseph H. Wherry

tionally smart. Because Eagle had not long been dead, Coyote thought his feathers would make better people than the old race, who were made of dust and dirt.

Coyote owned a roundhouse (the same kind of dance house still used today in several places), so he and his friends spread Eagle's feathers all over the floor in pairs. This done, they sat down to wait. When four uneventful days passed, Coyote decreed they would fast for eight days. Still nothing happened. Coyote then decided they all should lie down on the floor with their backs toward the fire. Again nothing happened; the feathers remained motionless. But all-knowing Coyote said they should try again for eight days—this time lying on their backs with their heads toward the fire, which burned in the center of the roundhouse directly beneath the smokehole.

During this last eight-day period Coyote asked for suggestions as to the best kind of hands for the new people. Coyote liked his paws but thought them unsuited to men and women. Kingfisher was also proud of his feet but agreed people needed better hands. Lizard, however, stoutly maintained that people could use hands like his and so it was decided that the new people would have five fingers on each hand. At the same time, it is said, the other physical characteristics of the new people were determined.

Now things started to happen!

Coyote and his friends observed small movements among the feathers toward the end of the third day. On the fourth day the movements became very lively. This activity continued during the fifth, sixth, and seventh days, and suddenly on the eighth day each pair of feathers became a man and a woman.

But there was a serious problem!

Each pair of feathers began to talk loudly and rapidly, but the pairs could not understand each other. Only the man and

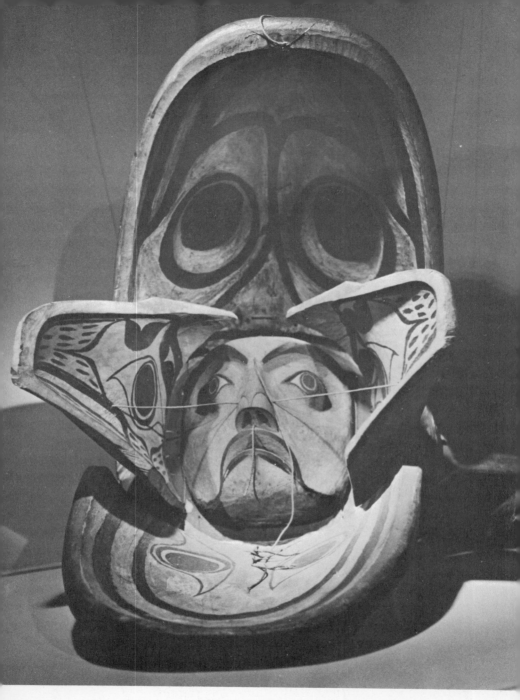

The human face reveals the inner spirit of the mythical Kwakiutl bird monster when the beak opens. Clever hinges facilitate movements of mask features for dramatic portrayals of traditional stories during winter ceremonies. AMNH by Joseph H. Wherry

woman from each original pair of feathers knew what the other was saying. It was a babel of tongues.

"We must find places for these new people to live," Coyote announced as he again called his friends into council. Together they decided that Coyote should name the country where each couple should live and that Kingfisher should mark down each place on the dirt floor of the roundhouse. This was quickly accomplished. Then Coyote stood and spoke with great authority:

"Each man and woman must now go to the land where you will live. That place will be your country. You will find much food and you will be happy and you will raise families."

Then a fantastic thing happened! The feathers vanished as suddenly each couple was transported to the country where it had been ordained to live. Thus, the Pomo couple, the Yuki couple, the Karok couple, and the first man and first woman of each neighboring nation were created and put in their own lands. Despite the disaster of the great flood and earth fire, the entire land was replenished with new people, and this is how the Indians came to Northern California.

In the beginning there was much to do. He Who Dwells Above, as the Coast Salish of the Northwest Coast call the Supreme Being, had many helpers who went about changing the earth from chaos, shaping the land, making mountains and rivers and lakes, and showing the few people how things should be done.

Sometimes these supernatural helpers of the Supreme One were mischievous, like Raven, who got into much trouble because of his tricks. Raven himself was changed from white to black for his misdeeds.

Thunderbird, whom we shall see first, was a friend of man

The Kwakiutl skill in fabricating compound masks is exemplified by this Thunderbird or Eagle mask. Sinew cords and leather hinges on the sides of the facepiece enabled the wearer to open the beak to disclose the inner human spirit when dramatizing myths like that in which Thunderbird showed a man how to build a house.
DAM by Joseph Wherry

in Totemland and a willing protector; he was also a teacher and, at times, a creator. Not that Raven was never helpful—he was, but he often caused nearly as much trouble as he cured.

We go then to the primeval forests of red cedar on the northeastern side of Vancouver Island where the Kwakiutl tell how the country of the Nimkish tribe was created and how the people learned to build houses in the very dawn of time.

Thunderbird Creates a River and Teaches the Kwakiutl How to Build Houses

Gyd'ee was a supernatural being who traveled all over, shaping the land in the proper manner. One day Gyd'ee was working in the Nimkish River valley. He was creating the homeland of the Nimkish tribe of the Kwakiutl nation when suddenly he came upon a man who was alone. The man rec-

60

ognized Gyd'ee as a supernatural being even though he was in human form. After a few moments, Gyd'ee asked the man what he would like to be.

"How would you like to be a mountain?"

"No, I do not think I would like to be a mountain," the man replied, "because I might break."

"Then would you like to be a large rock?" Gyd'ee asked.

"No," said the man, "I would not like to be a large rock because that really would not be any better than a mountain."

The human inner spirit of this Hawk mask shows its Haida origin by the drooping mustache, a common facial fashion among adult males in the Queen Charlotte Islands nation. When closed, the mask magically portrays Hawk, an eagerly sought crest. NMC by Joseph H. Wherry

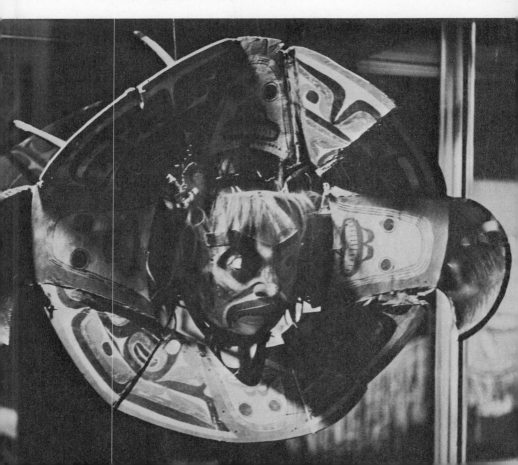

"Well then," Gyd'ee suggested, "perhaps you would like to be a river."

This possibility obviously interested the man very much.

"You will flow on forever," Gyd'ee explained, "and many fish and water creatures will be your companions."

The man thought this over carefully. Finally he replied, "Yes, I would like to be a river."

The supernatural Gyd'ee agreed that it would be so and he instructed the man to lie down on the ground.

"Be a river!" commanded Gyd'ee, and the man became a river which exists to this day on Vancouver Island, so long after creation.

Then Gyd'ee, the creator, went off about his business shaping the rest of the Nimkish land.

Soon a salmon came swimming up the new river. Becoming weary, the salmon swam up on the shore to rest a while; all of a sudden he changed into a human. Then one day the great flood came and covered all the lowlands and most of the higher ground as well. To escape the flood, the new man put his salmon skin back on and again became a salmon. To find refuge from the swift currents, the salmon-man swam upstream and went behind a high mountain.

When the flood subsided, the salmon-man swam back down to the river which Gyd'ee had created. Again he went up on the shore to rest and immediately he changed back into human form.

The salmon-man—and now he really was a human—decided to build a house. First he made an adz from a stone, and with it he felled several red cedar trees from which he shaped posts and timbers. As soon as the man set the corner and center posts, he decided to name his house Rhwarhwakesee. From that time all Kwakiutl have given names to their houses. The man discovered, however, that he did not know how to lift the huge roof-beam timbers, nor did he know how to set them in place on top of the corner and center posts.

Then suddenly the man heard a loud noise like thunder and an enormous bird landed on a nearby large rock.

"Oh, how I wish you were a man, because then you could help me build my house," the man said to the great bird. The man did not know that the great bird already knew that he needed help.

"But I am a man," the huge bird said as he lifted his beak upward to reveal his face. (In the same manner, to this day, the ceremonial performers lift the beaks of their masks when portraying supernatural birds during the winter dances.) "I have come to help you build your house," the great bird said with much dignity.

The house builder was truly astonished.

"I am Thunderbird, and I will help you set the roof-beam timbers in place."

Thunderbird then lowered his beak to cover his face, and fastening his powerful talons around a heavy timber, he flew upward with the sound of thunder and placed the heavy timber in place on the center posts of the house. Alighting after placing the other heavy roof timbers where they belonged, Thunderbird lifted his beak completely off his head, removed all of his feathers, and stepped forth in human form.

The supernatural man standing before the house builder was Gyd'ee, who had shaped all of the Nimkish land and had made the river, from a man, up which the house builder had swum when he was a salmon.

When the man's house was finished, Gyd'ee ordered the man who had been a salmon to put on the beak and the wings and all the feathers.

"Now you are Thunderbird," the man was told. "When there is danger, you will make thunder by flapping your wings and flying. You will do the same thing when a man

dies. By flashing your eyes, you will make lightning. With your wings folded, you will symbolize peace."

Then Gyd'ee and Thunderbird worked together for many days cutting down trees with their adzes, hewing timbers to support roofs, and shaping boards to cover the roofs and sides of the houses they were building. They built many houses for the Indians who would come to the land later to fill the cedar forests on Vancouver Island.

This is how the Kwakiutl learned to make houses.

Farther to the Northwest the creative agent of the Supreme One was Raven. To commemorate him, generations of Tlingit, Haida, and Tsimsyan carvers put the stories of his deeds on totem poles and his likeness on ceremonial masks such as those illustrated herewith. Into the darkness and chaos following the creation of man Raven intruded with good works wrapped up in a mischievous spirit.

Raven Brings Light to the Northwest Coast

In the time of long ago, darkness was everywhere beneath the clouds and the people were miserable. This was because a powerful chief far up the Nass River had a great carved box in which he kept the ball of light.

The tall Kwakiutl totem pole at the left came from Tsawadi village on Vancouver Island in 1914. Now preserved in Thunderbird Park in Victoria, the pole displays Thunderbird—Tsoona—at top; next down is a female cannibal giant with lips pursed for whistling; at bottom are two chiefs holding valuable "coppers." Joseph H. Wherry

65

Once owned by Chief Yailthcock of a Tlingit Raven clan, this mask was collected at old Klukwan village by Axel Rasmussen in 1931. The wearer moved the leather-hinged bottom part of the beak by sinew cords. Basically tan, the mask is trimmed with black and blue pigments. About 8 inches high and nearly twice as long, this humorous Raven's beak clacked and appeared to talk in reenactments of the story of how light came to the world of the Northwest Coast tribes. PAM by Joseph H. Wherry

One day Raven was in the Queen Charlotte Islands helping the Haida people when he heard about the plight of the people on the mainland. When his tasks were completed, Raven decided to fly to the headwaters of the Nass River. Gathering all of the small pebbles he could carry with him, Raven took off on his eastward flight across Hecate Strait. Whenever he became tired, Raven dropped a pebble which splashed into the sea below and became an island on which he could alight and rest. He dropped his small stones all the way to the mouth of the Nass River on the mainland of what is now British Columbia. The islands he made are still there today if you know where to look.

Now Raven knew that the powerful chief who owned the box containing light also had a daughter, and when he arrived at the headwaters of the Nass River he observed that the chief's daughter went every day to a certain spring for water. Consequently, after much cunning thought Raven decided upon a clever plan by which he would trick the chief. So he flew down to the spring and changed himself into a spruce needle floating on the water.

Presently along came the daughter of the selfish chief. As was her daily custom, the daughter drank several sips of the clear, cool water before filling the water containers for her father's house. As she sipped the water, the spruce needle washed down her throat. After a time it became obvious that the chief's daughter was going to become a mother. When the baby—who was really Raven—was born, the chief was delighted to be the grandfather of a healthy baby boy. The baby grew very rapidly because his grandfather stretched him every day, as was the custom of fathers who wanted strong, tall boys. Soon the baby was crawling all over the chief's great house and exploring every corner; he seemed to be searching for something among the many carved storage boxes which contained food, clothing, blankets, weapons, and ceremonial masks.

One day the baby boy began to wail and cry. Whenever his mother and his grandfather, the chief, tried to comfort him, the baby wailed more loudly. So the chief called the elders and wise men of his clan to council. He asked each of them what should be done to comfort the baby and make him happy. This was exactly what the baby wanted the chief to do. One after the other, the wise men tried to discover what

67

the baby wanted. Finally Raven caused one of the elders to say, "Give the baby the ball of light to play with—that is what he wants."

The chief then ordered his servants to bring him the great carved cedar wood box from its place near the wall. After lifting the lid of the box, the chief took out the precious ball of light and placed it on the floor beside the baby. Immediately the baby stopped crying and played happily with the ball, rolling it around the floor and talking baby talk. After playing for a while, the baby rolled the ball to one side pretending to be tired. Happy to see his grandson contented, the chief put the ball of light safely in its box. The baby did not cry again.

Now for the first time since the baby began to crawl about, the household could sleep. Every day the baby was given the ball of light to play with, and every day his grandfather stretched him and helped him to grow stronger and taller. All this time the baby was secretly scheming. As he played with the light ball, he planned how he could escape and fly away with the magic daylight. Because the smoke hole in the roof was never open when he played with the ball of light, the baby decided that he would watch for the door to be opened.

One day during the season of eulachon fishing when people were going to and coming from the chief's great house, the baby was playing with the ball. For a short time the door stood open, and while rolling the ball around, the baby managed to approach it without being noticed.

Suddenly the supernatural baby transformed himself into his true Raven form, clutched the ball of light in his talons, and before his mother or grandfather could interfere, flew through the open doorway toward the river. Downstream flew mischievous Raven until he became hungry.

Alighting in the top branches of a tall cedar tree, Raven watched the people fishing in the darkness. The only light to

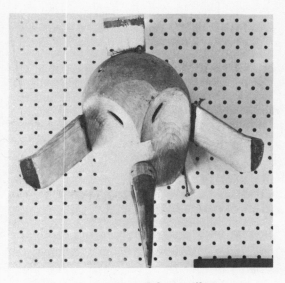

*From an unidentified Eskimo village some-
where on the western Alaska coast comes
this mask, which was collected without
data in the 1920s. Most likely the representation is of Crow or Raven's spirit.
Raven was not regarded as the bringer of
light by the Eskimo; considered rather
comical, he is portrayed in dances by participants who imitate his actions and
sounds. The black beak is removable; the
forehead is red, the face black.* University
of Alaska Museum

pierce the gloom was from their fish-oil torches. Finally,
when his hunger got the best of him, Raven called out loudly,
"Ga-Ga, give me some eulachon to eat!"

Busy with their nets in the Nass River, the people called
back, "Come down and get your own fish, you lazy one—we
are having plenty of trouble catching enough eulachon for
ourselves."

"I will let light out of the daylight ball," threatened Raven,
"if you refuse to give me some eulachon, and the bright light
will make you all blind."

The people thought about the matter. Then they said, "How could you get the ball of light, Raven? You do not have the daylight ball for it is a holy thing and it is safe in the great carved box owned by the powerful chief at the head of the river."

This made Raven very angry. The people evidently did not realize that *he* was the creator and that *he* was therefore supernatural. Holding the light ball so the people could see it, he called, "Now give me eulachon to eat or I will break the daylight ball and all of you will die!"

"Go ahead, Raven, and break the daylight ball," the people taunted. "We will then be able to see better while we fish." And they shouted with much laughter and mocked Raven.

With this disrespectful reply from the fishermen below, Raven clutched the ball tightly in his talons and with his strong beak pecked a hole in it.

All of a sudden light flashed throughout the entire Nass River valley! With cries of alarm the people fishing on the river below perished. To the last person the fishermen vanished, never to be seen again because they were all ghost people.

Now that light had come to the world of the Nass River, other people, real human beings, came from all around to fish for the eulachon, which are called candlefish today. The new people had plenty of oil for their night lamps and for seasoning their food. These new people were the first Indians in that region. They built cedar-plank houses, made dugout canoes, totem poles, and masks and became the great Tsimsyan tribes of the Nass, where many of them still live to this day.

The Haida of the Queen Charlotte Islands had a version of this story, too. In some traditions there were three boxes containing Sun, Moon, and Stars. Raven transformed himself first so as to be born a human baby with the knowledge of a higher chief, a fisherman, or another supernatural being. He could always see things others were unable to see. In another Tlingit version he transformed himself and flew upward through the smoke hole of the chief's house into the sky, where he released the light.

Raven also made the stars by breaking pieces off the Moon after releasing the Sun. Another time he disguised himself as a Crow woman and traveled to the ends of the world. One day he saw his reflection in the water and was so revolted with his long beak that he invented the labret, a lip ornament, by breaking off the end of his beak and placing the piece in his lower lip. Labrets became popular throughout the northwest coast, so much so that masks were carved with labrets in the lip of the representation.

3

Migration Myths and Other Adventures

urviving myths relating the migrations of bands of Western Indians from distant places to the lands they occupied at the time of discovery by Europeans are rare. In most cases these myths revolve about hero characters and have become, therefore, hero tales; several of these are retold in a later chapter. Two migration myths of wide regional acceptance stand out, however. One is of the far Northwest, the other a long tale from California. The latter suggests an intriguing land somewhere in the Pacific Ocean where the "first people" worshiped a high being named Mu. That this conjures a famous land of the same name is evident.

As with so many of the ancient traditions, the myth retains only a skeleton of its original form and does not clarify how the mainland was populated. However, because of the scarcity of complete myths relating to migrations, this one bears attention because it provides a vague North American mainland beginning for linguistic relatives of the mighty Sioux nations of the plains. Again we go to California, where most of the Hokan-Siouan-speaking tribes have variants of the following myth. Just where the offshore islands were located is not known; perhaps they are purely mythical. Possibly the story could dimly relate to the prehistoric Indians known to have existed on the Channel Islands off the coast near Santa Barbara. It is unlikely that it could relate to the Farallon Islands because of their barren smallness. Nevertheless in light of the vagueness of time and distance in the mythological age, the peopling of vast areas in California as suggested in this myth contrasts most interestingly with Coyote's creation of people in the preceding chapter. On the other hand, this epic may be about the "first people" who met their doom and had to be supplemented with Coyote's new creation already related.

How the Hokan-Siouan Speakers Came
to the West Coast

In the dim and distant past the forebears of many of the California Indians lived on an island somewhere in the Western Ocean. The island was Elam and they worshiped a powerful god named Mu.

Bear Mother was the mother of fifty daughters and the head of the people and she had large fields on other nearby islands where crops were tilled. It was the habit of the daughters and the people to go in their canoes to the island where they tilled their crops during the day. Every evening they returned to their village on Elam where Bear Mother watched over the fires in all of the dwellings while her clan was working.

One time, while gathering seeds in their fields, the daugh-

Feather headdresses, dance skirts, and flicker-feather headbands keep time with nimble feet and the drumming from the chanting elders around the "center of the world" post. This is an annual occasion at Tsunúnu Shinal—Huckleberry Hill—in Pomo country. Joseph H. Wherry

ters and all of their kinsmen were attacked by the Rock Giants. The slaughter was terrible and only four of Bear Mother's daughters survived to be captured and carried off by the savage giants.

"Why do my daughters and all of my people fail to return?" Bear Mother asked herself when darkness came to Elam. "I will go to see why they are detained."

Because the distance was short, Bear Mother swam to the island where crops were tilled, and after a short search she found the mutilated bodies of her clan. In fact she found all of her people except four of her beautiful daughters. "The rock giants have done this terrible thing," she sobbed as she returned to Elam. "Perhaps my four daughters escaped and returned to the village."

A search of the village on Elam failed to disclose any survivors who could have escaped and returned home. "The Rock Giants have stolen four of my daughters," Bear Mother muttered. "I will get them back." And she went to work setting fishing baskets along the waterfront and then she secluded herself to watch the baskets. Presently a good-size fish swam into the snare and Bear Mother picked it up. In her lean-to she filled a large basket with water—a tightly coiled basket much like those still made today by the Yuki, Karok, and Pomo Indians. Into the basket Bear Mother placed the fish.

"In the early morning you will be a baby," said Bear Mother, "and you must come to me and wake me up." After much medicine and incantations, Bear Mother lay down and slept.

Early the next morning the baby awoke and cried. Getting no response it crawled to Bear Mother and shook her. "Wake up, Bear Mother," the baby cried. "It is morning. Wake up!"

"Ah, you are a fine, strong baby boy and you will grow up quickly and rescue your sisters," Bear Mother said gently.

In just four days the baby had grown into young manhood. "Your name will be Nu-ku-wee, which means new growth," said Bear Mother.

"Yes, Grandmother," said Nu-ku-wee, as Bear Mother told him of the tragedy that had befallen his sisters and all of the clan. "Take your bow and arrows and go to the island where your sisters were working. Hunt for food and bring meat back here to our home."

Thus Nu-ku-wee went to the island where the seed crops were untended. Avoiding his kinsmen, the bears who were taboo for hunting and eating, Nu-ku-wee shot many rabbits which he brought back to his Grandmother Bear. "I have seen the footprints of the evil Rock Giants," he reported "and tomorrow I will go seek out the place where they have taken my four sisters. My mother is the Sea and the Sun is my father, which makes me very powerful. You will give me medicine, my Grandmother, and I will find my sisters and slay their captors."

After a peaceful sleep, Nu-ku-wee arose with the dawn, went outside and prayed to his father, the Sun, and after breakfast he prepared to start on his quest.

"Take this hornet nest, my Nu-ku-wee," said Bear Mother. "It is powerful medicine as is this spear with which you were born." And suddenly there was a great spear growing from Nu-ku-wee's body. "Throw the spear," Bear Mother commanded. When the spear came back to earth, it flashed with fire, and then it returned to his body.

"My blessings go with you, Grandson—I will pray for your safe return." And Bear Mother blessed him and sent Nu-ku-wee on his dangerous journey.

First he went to the island where his people had been toiling when the Rock Giants attacked. Finding no trace, Nu-ku-wee got into his magic canoe and went to the mainland. Climbing to the top of a range of low mountains, he saw

From Port Simpson, British Columbia, this splendidly carved Eagle with three young no doubt signifies the Tsimsyan owner of this forehead mask was an Eagle clan chief. Copper was used on eyebrows; eyes and beak are outlined with black, brown, and red coloring. Beneath beak is another small eagle. Length is 22 inches. MAI by Joseph H. Wherry

many giants in the valley below. Seeing Nu-ku-wee coming toward them, the Rock Giants threw their spears and cut a large tree to ribbons.

"They have great power but I have more," Nu-ku-wee thought, and he became invisible. "Now I wish to see my lost sisters." And when he came to a stream, two of his sisters awaited him, for they knew their brother was coming.

"Come with us to the village where we will feed and hide you," his sisters pleaded. After a dinner of acorn mush, Nu-ku-wee greeted his other two sisters, and then he was hidden in a large basket.

When the chief of the giants came to see his four wives, he asked what was in the basket.

"Our uncle is asleep there," said some of the chief's children. "He is visiting us."

Assuring his wives that he would not harm their brother, the chief departed and went to the roundhouse, where he told the assembled giants that his brother-in-law was in the village. "Have him come here and tell us about his journey by the fire," the giants asked the chief, and a messenger was sent to the chief's house.

As Nu-ku-wee entered the sacred place, he was set upon and tied securely to the center pole at the edge of the fire. The giants fanned the flames toward him until Nu-ku-wee slumped forward as if dead. Then they left the roundhouse. Using his medicine, Nu-ku-wee straightened up as soon as he was alone, flexed his muscles, broke his bonds, and carefully crept to his sisters' house, where he washed and was hidden away.

Returning to the roundhouse, the giants knew that Nu-ku-wee was alive and safe.

"Tomorrow we will invite him along on the hunt," the chief schemed. "He will be our beater and we will have traps for him in the underbrush." The other Rock Giants agreed.

Now Nu-ku-wee knew his treacherous brother-in-law would try again to kill him, so he was ready for the first trap the next morning as he went ahead of the hunters into the underbrush. As he stepped into a small clearing, he heard the buzz of rattlesnakes. Killing them easily with flashes of fire from his spear, Nu-ku-wee tossed the dead snakes at the feet of the hunters when they arrived at the clearing.

Ceremonial masks often displayed clan and lineage crests on the Northwest Coast, and crests were often the booty of war. This Tlingit lineage-crest mask, called "Lord of the Hawks," is made of wood with a walrus-hide scalp piece, shell teeth, and copper eyebrows and beak. Hawk is always carved with a sharply hooked beak which curves back to his mouth. UMUP by Joseph H. Wherry

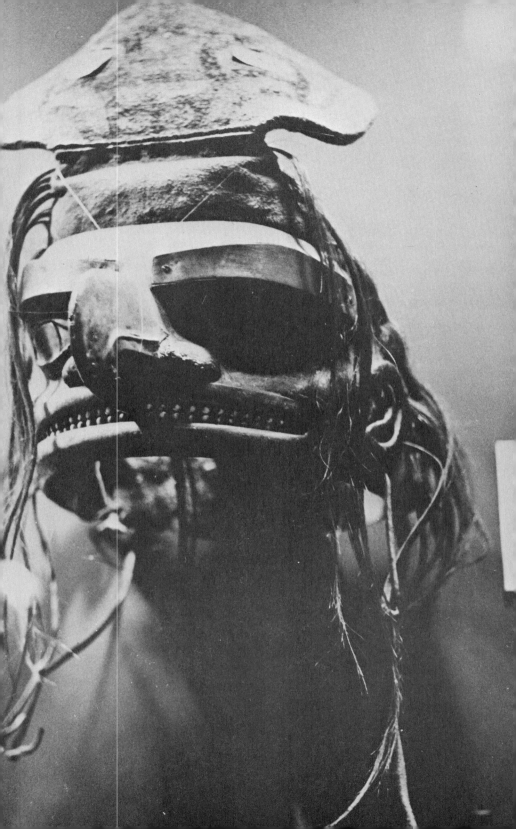

Soon he was face to face with two bears, but he quickly put them to flight with flashes from his spear. Nu-ku-wee could have killed the bear men but he would not commit a taboo against his kinsmen. Next a pair of cougars charged him. These he killed with two well-aimed arrows. Unknown to Nu-ku-wee, the hunters had gone around to the opposite side of the deep forest, and as he stepped out onto a plain, the giants unloosed their arrows at him, but each one fell harmlessly. Holding the medicine spear before him, Nu-ku-wee challenged them to shoot more arrows and soon all of their arrows were within his reach.

"Now I will use your own arrows against you," Nu-ku-wee shouted, and he launched all of the giants' arrows back at them with such accuracy that only the chief and a few giants escaped into the forest.

"Drive the giants into the open," Nu-ku-wee ordered as he shook the hornet nest. The hornets drove out all of the giants except the chief. Slaying the few giants took only a minute and then he went back to his sisters who were expecting him.

"I knew you would be here," Nu-ku-wee said to the chief as he slew him despite the cowardly cry for mercy.

"We are free forever," his sisters shouted. "Take us and our children home with you, Nu-ku-wee."

"I will, but first I must find Keb Muti, the high chief of the Rock Giants," Nu-ku-wee explained. "Wait here," he ordered as he started for the high Sierra.

As his sisters watched, Nu-ku-wee soon discovered he was surrounded by howling Rock Giants who showered him with arrows. Again he held his spear before him and the arrows fell harmlessly.

"Now I will use your own arrows against you as I did your kinsmen this morning," Nu-ku-wee shouted. Again most of his enemies were slain. The few who escaped were driven into the open by his hornets and Nu-ku-wee killed them with

80

his spear. Then he went back to his sisters who had prepared a fine feast for him.

"Only one enemy remains, my sisters," Nu-ku-wee reported exultantly. "Keb Muti still lives, but I will find and slay him," he said as he went off again toward the high mountains.

On his way he stopped for rest and refreshment at the roundhouse of the wolf people who were his cousins. From them he found the way to Keb Muti's cave. "Stop and rest and eat with Squirrel as you journey," the wolf people suggested as Nu-ku-wee thanked them for their hospitality.

"You must rest awhile," said Squirrel as Nu-ku-wee ate the tasty pine-nut mush set before him.

"No, I must hasten," Nu-ku-wee replied, "for as long as Keb Muti lives, all people are in grave danger. I dare not sleep until I have killed him." And Nu-ku-wee hurried on. He stopped only briefly at the house of White Goose Man but vowed he would return.

On the side of a mountain, high above the central plain, Nu-ku-wee spied a cave, and as he watched Keb Muti strode forth with a savage roar. Even as the high chief of the Rock Giants raised his arm to launch a spear, Nu-ku-wee threw his medicine spear. Straight to its mark it flashed and burned its way into the soft flesh beneath the upraised arm of the terrible Keb Muti. Flame flashed and Keb Muti pitched forward, mortally wounded, and came crashing down the mountainside with such force that the valley shook with a violent earthquake.

"All of my enemies are destroyed," Nu-ku-wee said thankfully as his flame spear returned to his body. "Now before I return to my four sisters I will ask White Goose Man for his two lovely daughters for my wives."

Returning to the house of White Goose Man, Nu-ku-wee found Coyote there on the same quest.

"To settle the argument," said the wise mother of the White Goose daughters, "let there be four trials. Tomorrow we shall determine who is the best hunter."

This was agreeable, and at the end of the day, as Coyote arrived without game, Nu-ku-wee returned with a fine deer, a present from Wolf, who was happy to help Nu-ku-wee defeat Coyote, whom he considered a fool.

"Today we shall see who can bring the most pine nuts," said the mother of the White Goose daughters.

"I will ask Squirrel for help," thought Coyote as he trotted off to the forest.

"I will help you," Squirrel said to Coyote. "Just climb a tree with many pine cones. Select a well-filled limb and crawl backwards out on that limb. Then with this sharp knife cut the limb off and you will have more nuts than you can carry."

Doing as he was told, Coyote cut a limb off and came crashing to the ground. As Coyote slept, Squirrel gave Nu-ku-wee a huge burden basket full of nuts. Hurrying back to the village of the White Goose people, Nu-ku-wee was declared the winner after a feast when Coyote returned empty-handed.

"On the third day Coyote and Nu-ku-wee will have a race," declared the White Goose mother much to Coyote's delight. Coyote knew that Nu-ku-wee had been born a fish in the sea, but the victor over the Rock Giants was confident he would

A Tlingit shaman at Point Lena, Alaska, owned this mask, which was collected by George Emmons in 1919. About 13 inches high, this excellent carving has snail-shell teeth, is painted black, blue, and red. Most likely representation is that of the woman who married the Frog Chief and thus became the female founder of the Frog clan, a myth particularly popular among the Tsimsyan. Note the nine frogs surrounding the face and a tenth issuing from the mouth. MAI by Joseph H. Wherry

win, even though he knew he was not a great runner like Coyote.

"You must race all the way to the sunrise in the East and return here," the two rivals were told.

Coyote was so anxious to display his speed that he failed to await the starting signal, and Nu-ku-wee seemed to fall farther behind no matter how hard he ran. As he was about to despair he heard a call from the sky: "Let us help you."

As he looked up, many blackbirds swooped down, carried him aloft, and flew with him almost to the sunrise where they put him down. This enabled Nu-ku-wee to arrive at Sunrise only a few strides behind Coyote who, though tired, was certain his great speed would take him back to the start far ahead of Nu-ku-wee. As he ran back toward Sunset, Nu-ku-wee was picked up again by the blackbirds, who flew faster on the return. Near the White Goose village Nu-ku-wee was placed on the ground. "Thank you, good friends," he called to the blackbirds as he ran with all of his might to the home of the White Goose daughters. On his way he sped past the foolish Coyote, who was very tired.

Everyone in the village expected Coyote to arrive first, especially the father of the White Goose maidens. "Coyote has never lost a race," the father said. "I don't like him much, but he is sure to win."

"But here comes Nu-ku-wee," someone shouted.

"Nu-ku-wee has defeated that rascally Coyote," said the father as Coyote came hobbling into the village complaining of an injury.

As they feasted that evening, Coyote demanded a trial of skill for the fourth and last event. "I will shoot my arrows at you and you, Nu-ku-wee, will hurl your spear at me."

Coyote used his thick fur as a quiver, and the next morning he was at the appointed place with more arrows than Nu-ku-wee had faced at the hands of the Rock Giants.

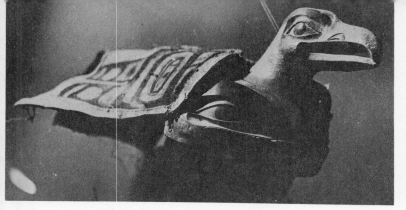

Tlingit ceremonial cap in the stylized shape of a mythical sea monster surmounted with a supernatural bird who guided people from Asia ages ago. It is not unlikely that the bird relates to Cormorant, the totemic crest of the chief of the Salmon Eater clan of Tsimsyan tradition. Woven veils were sometimes fixed to the front of such caps to obscure the wearer's identity during ceremonies or dramas. USNM by Joseph H. Wherry

Beneath the sheer bluffs of the Columbia River gorge trade flourished in prehistoric times between the Northwest Coast and the Plateau tribes. Down this waterway the Shoshoni "Bird Woman" led Lewis and Clark, and the prophecies of the old ones came true. Oregon State Highway Dept.

"Shoot first," Nu-ku-wee said, "shoot all of your arrows, Coyote, do not stop until you have loosed all of your arrows at me. Then I will hurl my spear at you."

As fast as lightning, Coyote shot his arrows at Nu-ku-wee, who stood quietly holding his spear before his body, and every arrow fell on the ground around him.

"How can Nu-ku-wee hope to hit Coyote with only one try?" the White Goose people wondered. "Watch!"

Grasping his medicine spear, Nu-ku-wee aimed and hurled it with all of his might. Straight to its mark went the spear, and Coyote, the foolish one who had tried once too often to confuse an adversary with a crafty trick, fell to the ground with the spear in his heart. The fire from the spear was Coyote's funeral pyre. After his marriage to the White Goose daughters, Nu-ku-wee took his wives back to the village of the slain Rock Giants, where his four sisters and their children waited for him.

"Gather your belongings," Nu-ku-wee instructed his sisters and their children. "We go now to our village on Elam to populate it again."

After making canoes, Nu-ku-wee set sail for Elam with his wives, his sisters and his nephews and nieces. Upon reaching land, the son of the Sun and the Sea brought his band to the village where Bear Mother awaited them. Again the village was populated. His sisters found their houses as they had left them on that morning when they had departed for the seed fields. After many days of feasting, Nu-ku-wee looked again toward the mainland.

The myth of the origin place of some of the Hokan-Siouan speakers does not go on from this time of reunion on Elam where Mu was the object of worship. Elam, however, is said to have been an island.

Of more substance is the migration tradition far to the North which relates how the Salmon-Eater clan came from across the foam-filled seas to the lands of the Haida, Tsimsyan, and Tlingit. The Thunderbird and Bear Mother traditions are of Asiatic origin, and the migration of Asiatics across the Bering Sea—or land bridge—during the Ice Age is well established by science.

Out of the Foam from Asia?

From out of the foam they came. This was the migration of the clan of Salmon-Eater which later evolved into the Eagle clans of the Haida, Tsimsyan, and Tlingit.

Salmon-Eater, also called Gitrhawn, was leading the seagoing canoes of his clan on a long journey occasioned by the great deluge which figures so prominently in all Western Indian lore. With only six loaded canoes remaining, Gitrhawn landed after many days on a strange shore inhabited by people speaking an unknown tongue. The people of this land were the Haida of the Grizzly Bear clan. The newcomers were well received and allowed to establish a village of their own opposite the Haida town. Gitrhawn's most precious possession was a cormorant-skin cap which he wore as a symbol of rank whenever the weather turned bad. His new village was somewhere in the northern part of the Queen Charlotte Islands a hundred or so miles southwest of modern Ketchikan. Food was plentiful and the migrants readily learned the island language.

Before long the nephew of the native Haida chief of the Grizzly Bear clan and Chief Gitrhawn's niece, Dzalarhons, were in love. According to the Haida custom, the uncles of

*An authentic war canoe of the far North-
west Coast—one of the few remaining—in
the Trail of '98 Museum in the first terri-
torial U. S. Court House in Skagway,
Alaska. The Tlingit craft is similar to those
made by the Tsimsyan and Haida. On the
wall are a hide dance shirt with a killer
whale design (left), a Chilkat-Tlingit
mountain goat ceremonial robe (center),
and a crest-marked ceremonial shirt
(right).* Alaska Travel Division

the prospective bride and groom conducted the formal ar-
rangements. The society was matriarchal, the common Totemland social organization. The groom's uncles carried the
bride, dressed in her ceremonial finery, from her uncle's
house to the shore, where they placed her on moose-skin-
covered boards between two dugouts which were lashed together. The wedding party then proceeded across a bay to
Chief Ka'it's Haida village, where the bridegroom waited.

Dzalarhons' clothing befitted a young chieftainness—two
fine sea-otter robes and an outer cloak of leather trimmed
with dentalia shells. (These tusk-shaped shells indicate that
the Gitrhawn clan was by this time well established, because
the northern tribes obtained this valued shell by trading with
Vancouver Island tribes two hundred or more miles to the

southeast. Tradition explains that dresses or skirts were unknown "in the old days," so the princess wore leather trousers
as was customary in ancient times on both sides of the North
Pacific Ocean.)

After the wedding festivities, the bride and groom retired
to their house, where the groom lay down to sleep. Dzalarhons did not rest, however, but was required to hold a lighted
pitchwood torch over her husband as he slept. When the
torch burned short, she protected her arm with her fine
leather robe, which was badly burned by sunrise. The
groom's uncles rebuked him for such rudeness to his bride
and warned that this would surely cause trouble. Chief Ka'it
knew Gitrhawn's clan would not look lightly on such humiliation of their chief's niece.

The bridegroom was unrepentant and, after several more
nights, all of Dzalarhons' fine sea-otter skins and leather garments were burned. When her nakedness was discovered,
one of the Grizzly Bear clan elders offered Dzalarhons a
Haida bearskin robe. This she refused. Stepping outside
without clothing, she met her own uncles, who were approaching with food and gifts to the groom according to the
Salmon-Eater custom. When Dzalarhons told the indignities
she had suffered, her uncles hastened to Chief Gitrhawn,
Dzalarhons' uncle.

Soon warriors of Dzalarhons' clan arrived. When Gitrhawn's warriors could not find Dzalarhons, they attacked
the Grizzly Bear clan village. Gitrhawn's forces prevailed
and then began to search for their lost princess. Eventually
they discovered a stone statue of a young woman whose legs
straddled a creek which seemed to be flowing from her—the
living waters, a symbol of fertility. Chief Gitrhawn knew this
statue was his lost niece, Dzalarhons, who had been so
shamefully treated by her groom, the Haida clan chief's
nephew.

Swaixwe masks were owned by Coast Salish families on the south mainland coast of British Columbia and southeastern Vancouver Island. Usually carved of yellow cedar with protruding eyes and painted with red, black, and white to represent the swaixwe, underwater spirits who helped fishermen and had healing power. The two bird heads probably symbolize ducks. There may have been a protruding tongue on this mask, which has a movable lower lip. MAI by Joseph H. Wherry

Not long after these events, Gitrhawn's own son insisted on wearing his father's cormorant-skin hat on a fishing trip to the lake formed by the river flowing from Dzalarhons' stone statue. Because hereditary power descended through the female side of a family, it was very wrong for Gitrhawn's son to wear the hat. One after another the men led by the chief's son fell dead after being pursued by the fiery figure of a woman carrying a staff surmounted by a large copper-colored frog. When the frog was killed, a volcano erupted and destroyed the Haida village and that of the Salmon-Eater clan.

After a series of disasters and escapes, a lone Gitrhawn woman married a Tsimsyan chief whose people—in six canoes—had rescued her. This young Salmon-Eater woman had managed, during the volcanic eruption, to obtain her chief's cormorant-skin cap. When she bore her first son to the Tsimsyan Gitrhahla chief, she named him Gitrhawn, and in this way the name came to the Gitrhahla people in the Nass River country on the British Columbia mainland. This son became a great chief whose descendants went far up the Skeena River. Other descendants, Gitrhawns, migrated north into the Tlingit country and spread the traditions and name of Salmon-Eater whose clan came over the foam into southeast Alaska in ancient times. Some say the trip occurred after the flood.

As this family grew, the mother told her children to go back to the clan's first home in Haida country and take their grandfather a gift of food. Two sons and a daughter started for the Queen Charlotte Islands in a canoe. Seeing an attractive beach, they stopped to rest in violation of the warning of their mother. A storm suddenly came up, badly damaging their canoe and destroying much of the food. For several days they were marooned. Then a strange man appeared whom they recognized as a supernatural being. The being changed into a great bird and took the young Tsimsyan Gitrhawns under his wings. In his mouth he put two stones; then he flew high over the water. Halfway across to Haida land the great spirit bird dropped a stone which became a large rock in the straits which can be seen to this day. He dropped another on an island beach near a Gitrhahla village where it, too, remains to this day if you know where to look. Finally landing the three young people in Haida land, the being warned them not to look until he had disappeared. The beat of his wings made a great roar and, unable to restrain her curiosity, the

The swaixwe are said to have taken a man who was dying from an incurable disease to their underwater spirit home, where they cured him and instructed him how to make masks. Powerful shamans who had swaixwe power could cure the sick. This mask has an extension beneath which served as a handle. The wearer looked through peepholes beside the bulging eyes. AMNH by Joseph H. Wherry

young woman peeked and discovered their benefactor was the giant supernatural Eagle-of-the-Sea, an aspect of Thunderbird. Knowing he had been seen, the monster eagle dove into the sea and appeared to sink.

After this the Gitrhahla clan people of the Tsimsyan carved stone eagles and took the great supernatural Eagle as their clan crest, which is still to be seen on totem poles and masks. With the increase of the family that began with the one remaining Gitrhawn princess, the Salmon-Eater tradition spread throughout the three northern nations, as did the Eagle clan crest and the story of the supernatural copper-colored frog on the staff carried by the fiery Volcano Woman. Of all the diverse Indians of the West, those of the Northwest Coast were the most devoted to the carving of masks, as the accompanying illustrations amply attest.

In the far Northwest honor and dignity were considered so important that the life force—or spirit—of a person who was dishonored through no fault of his own was believed capable of entering into a natural phenomenon. The natural phenomenon then became the vital outward manifestation of the dishonored or persecuted person, and punishment was visited upon those individuals who had perpetrated the indignities. Often entire families, clans, or tribes had to suffer for the rash acts of one or a few of their number. This was the aboriginal "eye for an eye" scheme of vengeance, because the world was a harsh place and those who tampered with custom and courtesy had to suffer the consequences. In some instances vengeance was visited even upon relatives of the wronged person when the former were deemed to have failed to honor the responsibilities of kinship.

Such was the situation when the fairest maiden of the migrated Salmon-Eater clan was given in marriage to a young noble of the Grizzly Bear clan only to suffer humiliation at the hands of her groom. Dzalarhons, having turned into a stone statue, still lived in spirit form and forced completion of the migration.

4

The Spirits of Fire
and Rain

uring the creation everything was imbued with life. Every tree, every plant, every mountain, plateau, and river had living spirits, and all creatures could converse with each other. Land, sea, and air creatures talked with men, and their inner spirits, or souls, were of equal vitality. All the animals could remove their fur or feathered coats, enabling each to perform many acts of magic. In some regions the ancient traditions tell of the time when the fire spirits dwelling in the mountains were selfish and would not help the people obtain fire with which to cook and warm their lodges. Similarly, the spirits controlling rain had to be dealt with, and magic gradually evolved into the shamanism so prevalent when the Europeans arrived.

How Indians Obtained Fire in the Northwest

The animals helped the Indians to get fire in what is now the state of Washington when there were many active volcanoes in the Cascade Mountains. Some say the war with the Fire Spirits occurred on Mt. Tacoma (now called Rainier), others say the fight was on Mt. Pilchuck, others say above the headwaters of the Skykomish River, and still others contend the great event took place high up on Mt. Baker or farther south on Mt. Adams. The exact location is lost in the mists of time, but it is certain that Grizzly Bear called a council. Everybody came: Beaver, Black Bear, Goat, Fox, Wolf, Woodpecker, Crow, Magpie, and all the others.

Fox ran around in circles the way he always does. "Did you bring all of your bows and arrows?" he asked everyone as they entered the council place near Grizzly Bear's lodge. "Did you bring your darts?" Fox asked Porcupine as he came ambling into the circle.

"Of course I brought my darts," Porcupine answered. "You see me wearing my coat, don't you?"

Fox spotted Wren, who was dragging his long bow behind him. "How can a little fellow like you shoot such a long bow?" he asked with his hand over his face to conceal a grin.

"Fox," said little Wren, "you go run a long way off and I'll shoot you."

Fox laughed as he ran a long distance, almost so far that he could not be seen from the council circle. Standing on a mound, Fox chuckled as he waited for the arrow to come. All of a sudden he felt a sharp pain as an arrow pierced his side and the point came out on the other side. Running back to the council circle, Fox went up to Grizzly Bear. "I found the best arrow shooter in the world," he announced. "Little Wren, Stilpakad, shot an arrow through me from a long, long distance. Now pull the arrow out of me and send warriors to bring Wren here."

Soon Wren and his grandmother were brought before the council. When told that he must shoot arrows high up where the Fire Spirits lived on the mountain, Stilpakad said, "That's too big a thing for me to do."

"I will show you how to do this great thing," Stilpakad's grandmother said, and they climbed to a hilltop from whence they could see the glowing crest of the mountain where the Fire Spirits lived. Stilpakad dragged his long bow up to the horizontal position. Then his grandmother, Kle-atlad, who was even smaller, climbed up Stilpakad's leg and up his body to his head. Raising her arm, Wren's grandmother pointed to a place high up near the crest of the mountain. "Now shoot," she cried, and Stilpakad pulled the bowstring back four times and let the arrow fly. As the arrow flew through the air Kle-atlad clapped her hands together four times, and the arrow went high, high, high, high and pierced the ground right in front of the Fire Spirits.

"Now shoot many more arrows up on the mountain toward the first arrow," said Wren's grandmother, who was a powerful shamaness. While she clapped her hands, Stilpakad shot arrows as fast as he could nock them to his long bow. After many arrows poor Wren was very tired, but there was a ladder of arrows reaching from the valley to the abode of the Fire Spirits.

"Now follow me." And Kle-atlad started climbing with Sta-ku the Beaver right behind. Beaver was a fast climber and, passing Wren's grandmother, he reached the glowing crest of the mountain before all the rest. Leaping from the ladder, Beaver rushed toward the glowing embers at the edge of the crater, but the Fire Spirits attacked him and hit him so hard he rolled over and lay still. Thinking Beaver dead, the Fire Spirits started to skin him. They skinned him on one

96

A realistic portrayal of an old man is the
mark of this Haida mask from old Skide-
gate village in the Queen Charlotte Islands.
The lower lip and eyelids are movable.
USNM by Joseph H. Wherry

side but Beaver was only playing dead, and when the Fire Spirits rolled him over to skin the other side, his skin instantly stuck back on him. By the time the Fire Spirits had skinned Beaver's other side most of the people were near the top of the ladder of arrows, and they jumped to the ground and attacked the Fire Spirits with their arrows, spears, and war clubs.

So furious was the attack that the Fire Spirits left Sta-ku for dead. Teke-te-katch the Woodpecker joined the assault with his strong beak and Magpie used his sharp eyes to search out all the Fire Spirits. Goat, who was at home on the rocky mountain top, Fox and Shweet-lai the Wolf fought with skill. When the battle was at its climax, Beaver put on the rest of his skin, ran to the glowing embers, and picked up as much fire as he could carry. Back to the ladder of arrows Sta-ku ran, but as he began his long descent, Grizzly—who should have been leading the attack because he had called the council—and Black Bear started to fight. Still on the ladder, the Bear cousins were insulting each other and arguing over which looked the worst. Soon they were engaged, tooth and claw, on the ladder of arrows, and they fought so hard that they broke the arrows they were standing on and they fell, causing everyone else to fall. Down, down, down through the arrows they fell, all of them tumbling down together.

Sta-ku the Beaver, however, kept his wits about him. Clutching the precious fire he had captured, Sta-ku jumped and landed in some ferns in the valley, which broke his fall. Quickly he went to a big hollow cottonwood tree where he put the glowing embers.

"This soft, dry wood will keep the fire burning," Sta-ku the Beaver said. "Now we will always have fire when we need it."

Because all animals and Indians talked to each other, the Indians heard about the capture of fire during the battle with

98

the Fire Spirits. So all the Indians had to do was to go to the hollow cottonwood tree and get some fire. In their lodges for a long time they kept their fire glowing, between cooking meals, by using dry rot from hollow cottonwood trees. In due time the Indians learned how to strike sparks into tinder by seeing how Thunderbird's lightning started fires. This is how Indians obtained fire when the world was young.

The tamanawis—guardian spirits—of the great Cascade peaks fought against each other during the primeval ages when the world was still being formed after the first creation. From time to time the volcano tamanawis of Mt. Hood in Oregon and those of Mt. Tacoma in Washington hurled fire and molten lava at each other with such fury that piles of lava were scattered over wide areas of these two states where they remain to this day. On one occasion, the old and wise ones say, the tamanawis of sacred Mt. Tacoma became so enraged at Mt. Hood that Tacoma's aim became inaccurate and many of the rocks and much lava fell short into the Columbia River at the Dalles. This is how the shallows were created in the great river of the Northwest. Another time a great priestess became involved in the feud among the volcano tamanawis.

Mentonee and the Mountain Spirits

From the beginning of time the Chinook tribes revered the Fire Spirit of Mt. Adams and the Storm Spirit of Mt. Hood. From peak to peak there was a mighty rock bridge on which there was a massive altar presided over by Mentonee, high

99

Made by a Haida of Massett village in the Queen Charlotte Islands sometime prior to 1890, this exceptionally realistic mask has eyes which move by strings, and may represent a white woman. The hole in the chin probably held a labret. RLMA by Joseph H. Wherry

priestess of the Great Oversoul. Each year the tribes came to bring their offerings to Mentonee, who maintained the altar fires and gave direction to the great potlatches. Mentonee's great beauty was her downfall because she had spurned the love of the Storm Spirit and Fire Spirit for many years. Jealous of each other, the two tamanawis began to fight just as had the tamanawis of Mt. Tacoma and Mt. Hood ages before.

100

From Mt. Hood the Storm Spirit let loose great winds, lightning, and clouds of snow containing masses of uprooted trees and rocks. All this the Storm Spirit flung at the Fire Spirit of Mt. Adams, who retaliated with fire and lava. The tribes fled but Mentonee remained at the shrine, faithful to the Great Oversoul, and kept the altar on the bridge of rocks, unaware that a young warrior stood guard close by. Hidden from her view, the young warrior had loved Mentonee for so long that his passion overcame any fear despite Mentonee's spurning of his love because of her devotion to her sacred obligations.

As the conflict between the Fire and Storm tamanawis reached its climax, the jealous spirits ventured from their mountain strongholds and advanced toward each other on the bridge of rocks. The spirits met in the center of the rock bridge hurling all of their snowstorms and volcanic storms at each other. The fury of the conflict caused an earthquake which broke the bridge of rocks. As it crumbled, the young warrior leaped to the altar and took Mentonee in his arms, and as they looked into each other's eyes and embraced, the colossal bridge of rocks exploded and came thundering down into the valley of the Columbia River. Mentonee and her faithful lover were buried forever beneath the millions of tons of granite and lava. The waters of the great river boiled and steamed as they washed the sides of the gorge. Retreating to their fortress peaks, the rival Storm Spirit and Fire Spirit watched in dismay at the destruction their foolish jealousy had wrought—they had destroyed the unattainable object of their affection.

This is why Mt. Adams no longer erupts and why Mt. Hood sleeps peacefully beneath its mantle of snow. Far below in the valley between the two peaks the Columbia still burbles and boils with white water to this day as it crashes over the rocky shallows on its wild rush to the sea.

101

* * *

In the great basin the elements threw down another challenge in the long past when drought stifled the land and parched all vegetation. All the rivers dried up and the lakes, deprived of the living waters, disappeared.

How Snake Brought Rain to the Shoshoni

All of the Shoshoni tried to find shade but there was none. The few surviving fish had burrowed into the mud on the lake bottoms and the water fowl had fled to the mountains where the animals had gone.

"We will die," the people said to their chief. "What can we do to bring rain?"

"What can we do?" the chief asked the medicine man.

"I have performed all of the rituals," the shaman replied. "The spirits have closed their ears to our prayers and their eyes to our suffering. Only the small animals with homes far beneath the ground are safe from the burning heat."

Far beneath, a brightly colored snake heard the medicine man and he listened to the people crying for water. "I will help them," the snake said, and he crawled to the opening at the end of his long tunnel.

"I can bring you rain," the snake said to the medicine man. "The clouds far up in the sky contain ice, and if you fling me up there I will cling to the clouds with my scaly skin and scrape some ice loose. The ice will fall and become rain."

"That sounds good," said the chief to the medicine man.

"But you are so small," the medicine man said to the snake. "How can you scrape enough ice to bring rain? I am a powerful magician and all of my rituals have failed."

102

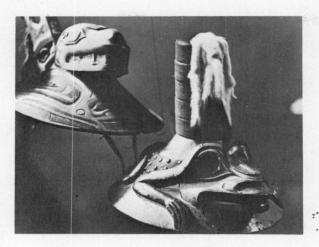

Tsimsyan traditions of a prehistoric migration out of Asia had counterparts in the neighboring Tlingit country. At right is a Tlingit chief's ceremonial hat decorated with a huge copper-trimmed frog, which relates to the copper frog accompanying the fiery figure of a woman in the Tsimsyan "out of the foam" story in Chapter 3. The five woven rings on the frog's back indicate the hat's owner had given five potlatches. The hat at left, also Tlingit, carries a figure of a sea monster, probably Killer Whale, judging from the holed fin. UMUP at left, OPM at right by Joseph H. Wherry

"You do not understand," said the snake. "You must have faith in my wisdom and magic. I will stretch from my small size to great length so that I will cover the sky from the North to the South. Throw me as high as you can and you will see. Believe what I say."

Urged by the people, the chief prevailed upon the shaman to do as the snake directed, so the shaman picked up the small snake and threw him with all his might up into the sky. When the snake had risen to the highest clouds which were without color to the people on the ground, he straightened out and stretched across the sky. Grabbing hold of the blue

Tribes from all over the Northwest gather every July Fourth for the pow wow hosted by the Flathead Indians at Arlee, Montana. The bison are gone, but tipis of canvas and an occasional hide spring up, papooses snuggle in cradle boards, braves paint, some of the old ones bring out the treasured sacred medicine bundles, the drumming starts, and everyone has a good time—even the palefaces. Montana Highway Commission

clouds with his scales, the snake arched from the South to the North end of the sky. Now the snake made his stretched body change to all the colors, and this, together with his scratching against the blue clouds, loosened vast amounts of ice crystals. Falling toward the ground, the ice crystals were

104

melted by the heat of Sun, and when they reached the people they fell as rain.

The snake kept moving and his body glowed with all the colors of the world. All that the Shoshoni could see was the rain. All of the plants and trees drank to their limit as did the dry stream beds which again flowed into the low places. Deep in the dried mud the fish came back to life and the desert animals and birds returned to their familiar haunts. When the thirst of the people and the land and that of all living things was quenched, the snake relaxed and rested. No longer did it rain, but the snake remained in his new home. When the weather cleared, the colors of the snake could be seen again.

"See," the people shouted as they danced, "the snake is staying in the sky and he is glowing with all the colors of the sky and world."

"He has bowed himself from the North to the South," the chief observed.

"He has become a rain god," the shaman replied. "Now we must make new dances and prayers to use whenever we need rain."

And that is how the rainbow came to be. To this day the Shoshoni remember the Rainbow Snake. His worship spread far and wide. So it was in the time of long ago when human beings and all of the animals conversed one with the other.

Farther to the south on the mesas the Pueblos have another tradition of how rain was brought to a dying earth. Versions of the story are told in all of the Pueblos, but that of the Zuni is the most exciting.

Ahaiyuta Slays Cloud Eater
and Brings Rain to the Pueblo Indians

In the dawn of time a monster named Cloud Eater took up his abode in the East on a mountain top. Taller than the highest mountain, Cloud Eater's mouth could reach all the way to the West. His appetite was voracious and his food was the clouds. Sometimes he was more hungry than other times, and when this was so, the entire land received no rain. Then the fields of maize withered and died and all of the animals starved. Only the people who had stored food could survive, but they also suffered. Many warriors had searched for Cloud Eater but none had the proper medicine.

Far toward the West, Ahaiyuta lived with his grandmother on the heights of Maize Mountain. Strong as his father, the Sun, and as fast as the deer, Ahaiyuta yearned for the time when he would be a great warrior. One day he went to his grandmother with a request.

·"Give me a task to do so I can become a man and take my place in the council circle," he pleaded.

"There is a great thing to be done which no man has ever been able to do," Grandmother said with a tone of warning.

"I am not afraid of the hardest task," Ahaiyuta replied. "Tell me what I can do."

"You must slay Cloud Eater so our people will no longer suffer from lack of rain, sometimes for many seasons," Grandmother directed.

"Who is Cloud Eater?" the boy asked, and his grandmother then told him how Cloud Eater had kept the people in poverty as long as anyone could remember.

"I will slay Cloud Eater, my grandmother." And the lad fetched his strongest bow and his longest arrows.

"First you must find Cloud Eater, my grandson," the old

The fire spirits of Oregon's Mt. Hood have
been silent beneath year-around snows for
hundreds of years, but the lava thrown in
the mythical wars with Washington's Mt.
Adams and Tacoma is evident in the Pacific Northwest. Frog Lake mirrors the
former volcanic peak. Oregon State Highway Dept.

Fire was the first supernatural gift. Many Navajo women bake their round loaves over an open fire in the traditional way.
Flagstaff Chamber of Commerce

woman said, and she went to a basket and removed four feathers.

"See these feathers. You must wear the red feather in your hair; it will guide you in the right direction. This blue feather has powerful medicine and will enable you to talk to the animals and to understand them. With the yellow feather in your possession, you can make yourself as small as the tiniest animal."

"But what is the black feather for?" asked the boy.

"That is the most powerful of all of the four feathers which are great treasures. You must guard them carefully and never let them out of your possession. The black feather, Grandson, will make you strong enough to accomplish the great thing you must do."

Early the next morning Ahaiyuta stuck the red feather in his hair, bade his grandmother farewell, and strode off to-

108

ward the East. All through the heat of the day he traveled as the red feather directed. The farther he went, the hotter the air became and the sparser the desert growth. The ground became more parched and there were large cracks. For several hours he had seen no animals, when a mole suddenly popped out as Ahaiyuta stepped near the entrance to his underground home.

"Can you tell me where Cloud Eater lives?" Ahaiyuta asked as he put the blue feather in his hair.

"Cloud Eater's home is just a few days' journey to the East, but you must be careful. He has killed all animals and plants, and if he sees you, you will be dead," said Mole as he scanned the horizon. "I would be dead too, but my home is underground where it is safe."

"I can go through your tunnels to Cloud Eater's pueblo," Ahaiyuta said, "and he will not see me."

"You are too big," Mole chuckled, but as he watched, Ahaiyuta placed the yellow feather in his headband. Instantly Ahaiyuta became as small as Mole and he stepped into the underground passage.

"Ah!" exclaimed Mole. "You have powerful medicine. You must be brave as well. Follow me."

As he followed Mole, Ahaiyuta observed the caches of food and water with which Mole had prepared his subterranean refuge. Stopping frequently for food and rest, Ahaiyuta was cautioned by Mole to light no cooking fires. Mole did not like smoke.

On the fourth day of their underground journey, Mole stopped. "We will soon be under Cloud Eater's pueblo."

As Mole spoke, the ground shook and there was a rumbling sound. The walls of the tunnel shook violently and some stones loosened. Then as the tunnel twisted and turned upward and ended, the earthquake continued.

"Cloud Eater's pueblo is above us," Mole said to Ahaiyuta.

Great care is observed by the Pueblo tribes to perpetuate the many kachina societies distinctive to each village. Unfortunately, as lineages die out, a proper clan member is not always available "in these days" to be instructed and initiated into the ancient mysteries. Consequently, the specifics about the deities represented by these intriguing kachina dolls, which were collected in 1905 at Hopi, are lacking. Much older, they are (left to right) Muzribi, Holi, and Polik Mana. From the various symbols it is safe to assume these deities had fertility, cloud- and rainmaking responsibilities. RLMA by Joseph H. Wherry

These Jemez pueblo kachina dolls represent the following masked deities from left to right: Hahai-i Wu-uti, the maternal ancestor of all kachinas (the Hopi counterpart, Hahai-Wuhti, is also the mother of Water Serpent) has two eyes, but the right one is obscured by blue design. Malo is a male cloud deity, as indicated in part by the stepped design around the mouth. Note the single horn. Suypaior, an unknown deity believed to be female and associated with clouds, rain, and fertility from the round head, stepped tablita, rain symbols, and young growth shoots. (Note that the kachina mother wears the thick, wrapped-buckskin leggings, typical dress of most Indian women in Southwest region.) RLMA by Joseph H. Wherry

"He is moving around as he sleeps. We must be very quiet."

"I hear Cloud Eater's heartbeats," Ahaiyuta whispered as he stuck the fourth feather, the black one, in his hair. "Now I will slay him," he said as he felt tremendous strength flow to all parts of his body.

Stringing his bow, Ahaiyuta braced himself as he placed his longest and straightest arrow on the string. Pulling his bowstring back to its limit, Ahaiyuta aimed at the place in the ceiling from whence the sound of Cloud Eater's beating heart was coming. When he released his arrow with a mighty twang, there was a loud roar of pain and another terrible earthquake. The ground caved in and Ahaiyuta and Mole were buried in the mass of dirt and rocks.

The ground was still shaking when Ahaiyuta awakened. All around them was destruction—the gigantic pueblo of Cloud Eater was a rubble and the monster's body sprawled motionless across the surface in a massive heap.

"You killed Cloud Eater," Mole shouted as he danced for joy. "The earthquake buried you as the monster writhed in agony, but I dug you out. See your arrow sticking out of Cloud Eater's heart."

The two companions faced the sky which was growing dark. Soon the rain came and fell to the land all the way to the West.

"Our people will no longer suffer from the selfishness of Cloud Eater," Ahaiyuta shouted as he joined Mole in the rain dance.

"And you have become a man and a great warrior," Mole answered.

And so it was that drought and blight were conquered in the arid Pueblo country where Ahaiyuta is spoken of with reverence to this day.

5

Monsters and Giants

N extensive mythology about monsters of the land and sea was popular among all of the tribes in the West. Many of these stories are told today where some of the ancient traditions are still observed. Wise old men, some of them shamans, held their aboriginal audiences spellbound, and the aura of the supernatural permeated every daily activity. Supernatural influences permitted such dangerous creatures to exist and also guided the Indians in their conflicts with the monsters.

American Indians were, at the same time, realists and mystics. It was obvious to them that they needed to employ bravery and imagination to overcome natural phenomena which they could not explain. Every stone, bush, lake, stream, hill, valley, animal, and each of the elements was imbued with the supernatural. Mysticism enabled the Indian to maintain his perspective amid unexplainable realism. With this in mind we find the monsters a little less far-fetched.

113

Cannibal Giants of the Deep Forests

In northern California and western Oregon these creatures are called "Oo-mah," or Bigfoot. In the Puget Sound area and in British Columbia the Indians call them "Sasquatch," which usually is translated as timber giant. Some Indians call the creatures "Dsonoqua." Newspapers on the West Coast frequently report sightings of these elusive wild giants who are said to stand nine feet tall and more and to weigh upwards of five hundred pounds. Indians of the West Coast firmly believe in Sasquatch and say that the reason white men are unable to approach them is because "Sasquatch does not like the white man's smell."

British Columbia Indians have numerous myths about the cannibal giants, who are portrayed by masked dancers in the winter ceremonies. The Kwakiutl tell about a chief of long ago who warned his sons about the colored smoke in the mountains. One day the chief's sons were preparing to hunt mountain goats.

"Take this oil, mountain goat wool, comb, and smooth stone with you," said their grandmother. "If a cannibal giant attacks you, throw these things in his path and you will be safe," she instructed the young men, and each of them carried one object.

After crossing a ridge in the coastal mountains, they saw strange, brightly colored smoke rising through the trees in a valley.

"That must be a camp of the cannibal giants," said one of the chief's sons.

"Yes," replied another of the brothers. "I think we must

see these terrible creatures," said another, and away they went despite their father's stern warning.

On the way down the mountain the youngest brother suffered a severe laceration of his leg, but he thought nothing of so slight an injury even though the wound bled profusely. As they approached the place where they had seen the colored smoke, they spied a brush hut.

"We must be careful," cautioned one brother as they entered the gloomy shelter. Near the fire sat an enormous woman who was holding a large child. The big woman stared at them.

Suddenly the youngest brother realized the hairy mother was staring at the blood on his leg. "Scrape the blood off your leg for my baby," she growled.

The terrifying whistling Dsonoqua—the bloodthirsty cannibal giant of the forest— is portrayed on this Nootka or Kwakiutl mask. Also known as Timber Giant and by another Indian word, Sasquatch, the legendary creature is known in Washington, Oregon, and California. RLMA by Joseph H. Wherry

115

Seizing a small stick, the youngest brother scraped the blood from his leg and handed the stick to the cannibal woman. When the mother gave the stick to the baby, it was seized hungrily and licked clean. Now the brothers knew they were in the house of a cannibal giant and they planned how they could escape. To show their skill with their bows, the brothers shot arrows through a knothole in the door. One by one they ran outside to retrieve their arrows and then they fled into the forest.

Right on their heels was the cannibal woman, who stopped outside. Pursing her lips, she whistled for her husband. When they heard the loud whistle, the brothers knew they had almost been captured by a whistling Dsonoqua, and they headed over the ridge toward their village with the cannibal husband close behind.

"The cannibal giant is getting close," yelled the oldest brother as he remembered the smooth stone his grandmother had given to him. As soon as the pebble was thrown toward the monster, a steep mountain appeared and the brothers were able to get far ahead of the creature who had difficulty climbing the steep mountain.

After a time the brothers again heard the crashing and whistling of the Dsonoqua behind them. "I will throw Grandmother's oil on the trail," said the second-oldest brother.

Instantly the oil formed a vast lake behind them and the cannibal was forced to go far out of his way. When they were

About 13 inches high and colored black, blue, brown, green, red, and white, this Kwakiutl mask was collected by C. F. Newcombe early this century. The fierce visage is that of the omnipresent cannibal monster, Dsonoqua, but this particular mask is reported to have been used in wolf spirit dances and shamanistic rituals; possibly used in retrieving lost souls. PMBC by Joseph H. Wherry

about halfway to their father's house on the coast, the Dsono-qua was close behind them.

"Now it is time for me to throw the wooden comb on the trail," said the third brother, and when the comb hit the ground it miraculously turned into a huge barrier of wild crabapple trees. Caught in the tangle, the cannibal giant fought to free himself. As the brothers ran on, they heard the Dsonoqua thrashing about and whistling in anger. Eventually the giant's great strength enabled him to penetrate the barrier and, when they were nearing their village, he had caught up to the brothers.

"Now I will throw the wool of the mountain goat behind us," the youngest brother cried, and as he did, the roaring, whistling monster was engulfed in a fog so dense that the brothers were able to escape his grasp again. As they drew near, their father came out of the house.

"Father, the cannibal giant is chasing us," the oldest brother called. "Wrap a rope of shredded cedar bark around the house to prevent his entering!" When this was done, the four brothers and their father dashed into the house barely ahead of the giant. Unable to break through the stout cedar rope, the Dsonoqua stepped upon the roof and began jumping up and down. Suddenly a roof plank gave way under the weight of the monster and he thrust his head through the hole.

"Come back on the morrow, Dsonoqua," the chief ordered, "and bring your family."

Collected around 1896 by F. Jacobson from the Nootka of Clayoquot Sound on Vancouver Island, this mask represents the cannibal monsters who stole children and ate them. Worn in the Wolf Dance, which was characterized by a long, running step. Carved from cedar, the decorations were feathers with red and black paint. AMNH by Joseph H. Wherry

118

After a hearty meal of smoked salmon, the four sons were instructed to repair the roof. Then, as their father ordered, they dug a deep pit in the ground near the chief's fire. Planks were placed over the pit to conceal it.

"I will invite the cannibal monster family to sit on the planks," the chief explained. Four dogs were then killed and their internal organs were piled near the covered pit but their bodies were buried.

"Now put many rocks in the fire so they will be red-hot when our guests arrive," the chief ordered. Then the entire household retired for the night.

Around midday the air was pierced with much whistling. "The cannibals are coming," a servant reported. Wearing his finest goat-wool cloak, the chief met his guests at the door. Ushering the man, woman, and child Dsonoquas inside, the chief motioned them to sit on the planks near the fire.

"I have prepared your food for you," the chief told his guests as he pointed to the pile of guts beside the motionless bodies of his four sons. "Before you enjoy your feast, however, you must hear a story. I take my talking stick in hand," the chief announced, "and now I will tell you the story of my clan."

As was the Kwakiutl custom, the chief emphasized important parts of his story by pounding the talking stick upon the ground. After a short time the giant family dozed. Soon they were sound asleep.

"Now!" shouted the chief, and his four sons leaped to their feet and yanked the planks apart so swiftly that the Dsonoqua family tumbled into the pit. Just as quickly other members of the household pushed the red-hot rocks into the pit while the sons poured boiling water upon the cannibal giants.

When the Dsonoqua bodies were consumed by the inferno, the chief and his sons scattered the ashes to the North, East,

120

South, and West winds as the chief cursed the cannibal spirits: "From this time forth you will be mosquitoes."

And it was so. Ever since that family of cannibal giants was destroyed, the Kwakiutl have celebrated the Cannibal Dance and have carved many masks representing these wild monsters of the evergreen forests. The dances show the Indians how to protect themselves, and with the masks the shamans are able to project their own spirits into the houses of the cannibal giants to rescue the souls of Indians which have been stolen.

From the descriptions supplied by many Indian tribes, the timber or cannibal giants are similar to the legendary Abominable Snowmen said to inhabit the Himalaya Mountains. To the Bella Coola, whose territory was bounded on three sides by that of the Kwakiutl, the creatures were called "Snanaik," and females of the species prowled about Indian villages. Many a child was snatched from play, stuffed inside a basket, and carried off never again to be seen. A Bella Coola deity was the Sun. On one mythical occasion, the Sun shone so brightly upon the tears and mucus of a Bella Coola mother (whose girlchild was stolen by a Snanaik) that a manchild was born. The child grew miraculously in four days (a frequent supernatural occurrence throughout the West) and announced that he was born to rescue his half-sister.

Wearing ornaments inlaid with abalone shells and armed with a salmon spear, the Sun Boy set off to find his half-sister. When he heard the Snanaik approaching, the boy hid in a tree. Upon discovery, the boy was addressed by the huge female cannibal.

"How did you become so pretty?" the creature asked, for Sun Boy had red hair and his features were unusually handsome.

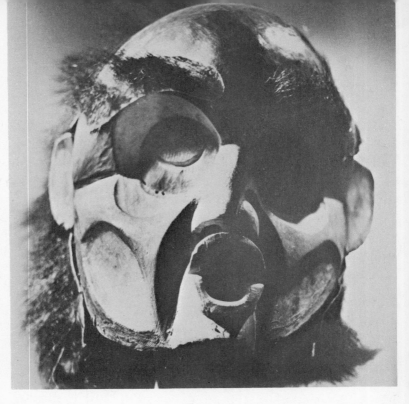

Another Kwakiutl mask showing the pursed lips of the fearsome creature called Dsonoqua and Sasquatch in British Columbia and Washington. About 14 inches high, this fur-trimmed example was collected at Alert Bay by D. C. Scott in 1922. NMC by Joseph H. Wherry

"You could be as beautiful as I am," replied the lad, "but I don't believe you would like the method."

"Please come down and make me as beautiful as you are," the Snanaik said.

"I will have to cut you with knives and you will suffer much," the Sun Boy replied.

"Do whatever you must," the hairy creature agreed, and the boy came down out of the tree.

"We must search for the knives," the boy said, and together they walked until the knives appeared. "Lie down here," the Sun Boy ordered, and the Snanaik did so. Placing one knife, blade up, beneath the creature's neck, Sun Boy brought the other knife down in a flash and the monster's head was severed from the body, but the boy had to pass his hand between the severed parts to prevent the supernatural reunion of the head with the body. In the cannibal's hut the Sun Boy found his half-sister, who was dead, but his miraculous touch restored her body and brought back the spirit of life. The little family was reunited when the half-siblings returned to their anxious mother.

Equally fearsome was the giant Goo-teekhl, who ravaged the villages of the Chilkat tribe of the Tlingit north of modern Juneau. So huge was Goo-teekhl that he often hurled large tree branches at hunters sitting about their campfire. Many children were lost to the creature too. Warriors learned that spears and arrows could not kill the monster, so finally the Frog clan prepared a firepit and tricked Goo-teekhl into chasing them. Once entrapped, the creature was bound with ropes and sinew nets and then the fire was started.

For several days the fire was fed with wood and eulachon oil until the cannibal giant was consumed. When the winds scattered the ashes, swarms of mosquitoes arose. Just as in the land of the Kwakiutl, the giant's thirst for human blood was transmitted to the insects in a supernatural manner. Perhaps this is why the mosquitoes in the far North are so large and ferocious. Tlingit mythology states that anyone who dreams of Goo-teekhl will have good luck.

Masks and totem figures of Goo-teekhl were fed daily meals of eulachon oil, and a few such figures are believed to still exist.

*   *   *

In the Queen Charlotte Islands the cannibal giants were real too. In a Haida myth one of the monsters was tricked into jumping into a lake which froze when the last of several brothers sang a spirit song. When the monster was burned with a fire built around his head, which was protruding through the ice, the ashes again turned into large mosquitoes. Many masks were carved of Mosquito, who was a valued guardian spirit. The insect's thirst for blood is symbolic of the immortality of the soul, and a shaman who is the protégé of Mosquito is able to heal the sick after purification and fasting. On the other hand, an unworthy shaman will cause affliction to a patient if he calls upon Mosquito's spirit.

The Sasquatches who harassed the Salish tribes on the east side of the "whulge" (Puget Sound) in Washington were called "Steet-athls," and were believed to live in caves in the mountains. (The same beliefs were held by the Salish tribes on the east side of the Cascade range, which they called the Kenkempkin.) Because they skulked about at night, the presence of these wild creatures could be discerned only by placing a stick in a mound of damp soil. If the stick was knocked down during the night but no tracks were left, the Steet-athls were known to have visited. Like the Dsonoqua of British Columbia, the Steet-athls communicated with each other by whistling; they also carried off children. Now they are said to be few in number, but as recently as 1912 a party of loggers near Chehalis, Washington, fought a pitched battle with some wild, hairy men of the forest who are believed to inhabit isolated areas in the Pacific Northwest.

Among the tribes of the northern Oregon coast, the timber giant was feared as the creator of red huckleberries, which if

124

Collected by George Emmons on Vancouver Island c.1900, this 15-inch-high mask is of either Haida or Kwakiutl origin and shows "the wild man of the woods"—Olala or Dsonoqua—or an unidentified water spirit. Black and red pigments were used with bits of bear skin. USNM by Joseph H. Wherry

picked and eaten at night, caused insanity. The female, called A-sin, the deadlier, was fond of stealing unguarded children. Shamans desiring to cause trouble would dream of A-sin, and then they could bewitch people and cause them to die.

In Apacheland Owl had many black arrows and a throwing club which returned after killing men until Coyote tricked Owl into a contest. Coyote killed Owl, took his weapons, and became a slayer and eater of men. Everywhere *four* was a magic number, as already observed in the Bella Coola myth about the child of the Sun and in the slaying of Cloud Eater in a previous chapter. In the Southwest, particularly,

125

four usually was connected supernaturally with the four directions. One of the most intriguing Apache myths suggests a reason for the mystical charm of eagle feathers, which were symbols of strength and bravery throughout North America.

Monsters of Apacheland and
Why Bat Has No Feathers

The Sun's second wife is the Old Woman who lives in the West according to the Jicarilla Apache. Their son was the warrior Jonayaiyin. Old Woman also had a second son, Kobachischini, whose father was Waterfall. In some versions of this myth, the two boys were regarded as twins although they were really half-brothers. The related Navajo have a similar tradition in the twin warrior gods, and the Chiricahua Apache call the monster-killer Child of the Water; the latter is the miraculously conceived son of White Painted Woman, of whom more later.

Jonayaiyin matured supernaturally in four days. His mother made him a bow and arrows and taught him how to use them.

"Now you will find the monster Elk in the desert far away in the South," his mother told him, and in just four giant steps Jonayaiyin was within sight of the cannibal Elk. Lizard offered the young warrior god the use of his skin as camouflage, but in four attempts Jonayaiyin could not squeeze into it. Then Gopher offered to help.

"I will burrow beneath Elk and chew the hair from over his heart," said Gopher, and swiftly Jonayaiyin's ally burrowed through the ground into the middle of the desert until

126

Made by a Haida to represent the mosquitos which arose supernaturally from the ashes of Cannibal Giant. Mosquito's spirit empowers a shaman to cure illness if he has been careful to fast and purify himself; otherwise this guardian spirit's power will have evil consequences. Some shamans "restored lost souls" with this power. An evil shaman could direct mosquitos upon an enemy with dire results. NMC by Joseph H. Wherry

he heard Elk's heart thumping, whence he burrowed upward.

"What are you doing?" Elk snorted, and Gopher replied, "I need some hair for my children." Soon Gopher had chewed all the hair away from the skin over Elk's heart.

"Now you go into my tunnel and shoot your arrows into Elk's heart," Gopher told Jonayaiyin when he returned. After four attempts the warrior god squeezed into the tunnel, and when he was beneath Elk he shot four of his magic arrows into the monster's heart. But instead of dying, Elk thrust an antler into the tunnel and pursued Jonayaiyin. As

127

he ran, Elk ripped up the earth, creating all the mountains in Apache country. Racing to the East in his rage, Elk was stopped by a web spun by Black Spider, and when he reached the South, the web of Blue Spider forced him to turn to the West, where Yellow Spider's web stopped him. In his desperation to catch his assailant, Elk turned to the North, where Spider of Many Colors had spun a web. Tired out and mortally wounded, the monster Elk fell dead. No longer would he destroy the Indians.

After giving Gopher and Lizard half of Elk's hide, Jonayaiyin hastened back to his mother and gave her the monster's antlers. "I have been singing for you, my son. The medicine bundle of cedar bark has been falling when you were in peril and rising when you were safe. Now when you have rested awhile you must destroy Giant Eagle who is carrying off the people. You must wear an elk skin for protection and carry an antler as a weapon."

Great Eagle lived in the West on a high mountain. In four great steps the young warrior god was beneath the home of Eagle and he knew the monster bird would try to carry him away. In turn he faced each of the Four Directions, and as he faced the East, the eagle finally swooped down and fastened her talons into the tough elk-hide cloak of the warrior deity. Swiftly Eagle flew up to her house and threw Jonayaiyin to her children, who would have blinded him had he not given them the blood of the giant Elk.

"When will your mother return?" he asked the eagle children. "When the rain comes," they replied, and armed with one of Elk's huge antlers, Jonayaiyin hid to await the return of his adversary. Soon he heard the thunder of Eagle's wings; the creature was about to land with a captive Indian. Raising his antler weapon, Jonayaiyin brought it crashing down on Eagle Mother's back just below her neck. Instantly she fell dead.

"Now when will your father come home?" he asked the eaglets, and they replied, "At the sunset." As the sun started down in the West, Father Eagle arrived and dropped an Indian woman and her baby into the nest. Swiftly Jonayaiyin killed the second giant bird as he had the first.

"Now I must prevent eagles from growing into large and dangerous monsters," the hero thought as he hit each of the eaglets on their heads with the antler. From that time forth, eaglets are smaller when hatched, and when fully grown they are no larger than the cannibal eaglets were when bested by the son of Old Woman and the Sun.

Jonayaiyin, however, was marooned on the steep mountain, so he gazed all over the flat land far beneath for a means of escape. Spying a large bat, he called, and after hesitating, the black creature flew up to the mountaintop. "I have destroyed the giant eagles and from this time eagles never will be able to carry people away from their homes. Carry me to the land below and I will give you many feathers."

"Yes, I will help you," old Bat Woman agreed. "Climb into my basket. Don't worry about the spider-thread handle; it is strong and has carried large animals in perfect safety. Be careful, though, and keep your eyes tightly closed or much harm will come to you."

"I will help you fill your basket with eagle feathers as soon as we fly to the foot of this mountain where the creatures lie." When the downward flight was ended, Jonayaiyin helped old Bat Woman to gather the feathers.

"Take your basketful of feathers to your home," Jonayaiyin suggested. "If you carry the feathers about with you, birds will steal them and you will have none."

"Yes, you are right," old Bat Woman replied as she thanked the warrior god and flew away. So happy was old Bat Woman with the pretty feathers that she forgot and carried them with her as she flew about her business. All of the

There were monstrous cannibal birds too in Kwakiutl lands on Vancouver Island and the mainland. After newly initiated members performed their first spirit dance before the elders of a Kwakiutl shamans' society, the masked cannibal dancers appeared. Cannibal Bird is always carved with a looped snout on the upper jaw of wide beak. Black, red, and white pigments are used with shredded natural red cedar bark to represent the feathered scalp of this wild-eyed creature. PM by Joseph H. Wherry

Extremely picturesque is this beautifully preserved Kwakiutl double mask portraying Raven or Hohoq (right) and the terrifying Cannibal Bird (left). Cannibal Bird was always worn to the front. Note Hawk's beak under Cannibal Bird's beak; this could be the owner's crest. Used in ritual meetings of the shamans' society. Long strands of shredded red cedar bark hid the wearer's own face. Collected by C. F. Newcombe in 1914, coloring is black, red, and white. PMBC by Joseph H. Wherry

birds took turns stealing the feathers and back she came three more times.

"You have had four basketsful of feathers," Jonayaiyin told her when she came back for the fifth batch. "I warned you to be careful. You are careless. You cannot have any more feathers." And from that time bats have had no feathers because old Bat Woman failed four times to guard her feathers.

In the Chiricahua version, this culture hero is Child of the Water, son of White Painted Woman and Waterfall; with the feathers of the monster eagles he created all of the birds. Brother to Child of the Water is Killer of Enemies; he liberated all of the game animals from a cave where they had been held by Crow.

There were monster beasts in the Cascade Mountains, too, when the world was young. Yakima mythology tells about the struggles between Coyote and Giant Beaver, who lived in the lake near Cle Elum just east of the divide where coal is now mined. Such monsters changed the land, and the Indians know how these things happened.

Giant Beaver Makes a River

Between the Swan and Flathead mountain ranges in northwestern Montana is beautiful Flathead Lake. This myth has Flathead-Salish, Nez Perce, Kootenai, and even Blackfoot overtones. The tradition is well known in the plateau interior of the Northwest.

In the lake, just south of the city of Kalispel, lived Giant

Mythical cannibal bird mask used by the Bella Bella tribe of the Heiltsuk division of the Kwakiutl. About 19 inches long with a scalp of bear fur, and worn low over forehead, this mask was used in shamanistic dramas. Collected by Franz Boas late in 1894. The bottom of the beak was hinged to open wide. AMNH by Joseph H. Wherry

Beaver, who was so immense that even a dozen warriors could not conquer him. It is said that he lived when a river flowed out of the west side of the lake many thousands of years ago. It was then that Giant Beaver constructed a dam across the opening in the lake because he was getting so large that the lake was too shallow for him. Ancient Flathead River dried up and the lake got deeper and deeper, and to keep all of his water, Beaver built another dam across the south end of the lake and he was happy.

Winters in Montana are cold and the snow gets deep. During one especially long, hard winter the snow piled up deeper on the frozen lake than at any time since. Toward the end of winter a warm Chinook wind came roaring into the valley of Giant Beaver and all of the snow melted in an unseasonably

132

warm night. Giant Beaver's dam across the south end of the lake was not high enough to contain all of the melted snow on the frozen lake and that which came down the surrounding mountainsides in avalanches and through the upper Flathead River, which empties into the lake on the north side. The inevitable happened—the dam broke and a new torrent carved out the present course of the Flathead River on the south side of the lake. Remnants of Giant Beaver's dam can still be seen at the south end of the lake. After this happened, some mountain bison are said to have come into the high valleys. This is what some of the Indians still say.

Today you can see buffalo in the National Bison Range about thirty miles south of Flathead Lake near Dixon and Ravalli.

When a young lad, the author occasionally swam in Osoyoos, a small lake on the Okanogan River a few miles north of the Canadian border above Oroville, Washington. Osoyoos, like Loch Ness in Scotland, is believed to harbor a sea serpent who makes sporadic appearances during storms. And there are others . . .

Lake Monsters

This is another ancient myth that conjures memories of my boyhood when I went fishing with the late Chief Pete Wapato of the Chelan Indians, a division of the Methow tribe, which lived around Lake Chelan in north-central Washington. Chelan mythology says that a monster lived in the area in ancient times before the fifty-two-mile-long, two-

133

According to an ancient myth, Giant Beaver dammed the south end of Flathead Lake in Northwestern Montana and changed a river's course. Montana Highway Commission

mile-wide lake existed. In those days the long, narrow valley was full of deer, bear, mountain goats, and elk, but the monster killed them so fast the Indians were starving.

Invocations to the nature spirits and to the Great Spirit above for help were effective, because the monster was mysteriously killed. Many years later the monster miraculously revived and renewed his onslaughts against the wild life and even threatened the Indians. Again the Sky Chief killed the monster and for a time the elk and deer returned. But the monster revived a second time and the Great Spirit came to earth again in answer to the supplications of the Indians. In his anger the Great Spirit cut the monster into small pieces and then he hit the ground so hard with his great stone knife that all the world trembled and an enormous cloud covered all the earth. So mighty was the earth's convulsion that mountains appeared. Between the ranges a great crevice was created into which the Great Spirit threw the remains of the terrible monster, and the Indians gave thanks for their deliv-

134

erance from the beast. Into the deep crevice flowed the water from the melting snows on the high mountains which the Great Spirit had formed with the crashing blows of his great knife. So deep was the new lake that it extended into the earth's center.

The monster's body was truly destroyed, according to the Indians—all except the great serpent's tail, which still lives and thrashes about, sometimes with such force that terrible storms and great waves appear without warning. All of this is true—fearful storms still come up like thunder on the slender mountain lake, often when the weather in the area is mild. Anyone who has lived near Lake Chelan knows this.

Old Chief Wapato knew this too, and sometimes when we were fishing we would paddle hard for the shore at Wapato Point near Manson. Sure enough, great waves would soon lash the lake into a frothing madness. In many places the bottom of the lake never has been found to this day, and the water in most of the lake is icy cold. Even modern whites admit the lake is dangerous.

In the old days of Chiefs Joseph and Looking Glass, the Wallowa Mountains in Northeastern Oregon were Nez Perce lands. Near Enterprise and Joseph, named for the brilliant chief, the score of alpine lakes were the haunts of numerous supernaturals. Oregon State Highway Dept.

* * *

Many Nez Perce regard Wallowa Lake in northeastern
Oregon as the hiding place of sea monsters—giant crabs and
even a great dragon. In early times buffalo and elk inhabited
the area, but when hunters approached, the beasts fled into
the lake where they would be safe. To venture upon the lake
was to court disaster because of the huge crabs.

There was a monster serpent in the lake, too. Once long
ago Chief Red Wolf led a large hunting party of Nez Perce
to the buffalo plains in Montana, where they were ambushed
by a superior force of their traditional enemies, the Blackfoot.
After many years of warfare the Blackfoot succeeded in driv-
ing the Nez Perce back to their camp on the west side of
Wallowa Lake; the Blackfoot warriors camped on the opposite side. During the night Princess Wahluna, Chief Red
Wolf's only daughter, slipped away. After crossing the lake
by canoe, Wahluna went into the camp of the Blackfoot,
where in council with Bloody Chief and his son, Tlesca, she
pled for peace. Soon Wahluna and Tlesca fell in love, and
after many moons a marriage was arranged. The two warrior
tribes would live in peace and hunt the buffalo together.

As Tlesca and Wahluna were crossing the lake one evening from the Nez Perce to the Blackfoot camp, the surface
of the waters erupted in a demoniac fury. From the shore the
startled warriors of both tribes saw a serpent raise his head;
then his scaly tail lashed out at the canoe carrying the royal
sweethearts. In one terrible strike, the serpent's tail crushed
the canoe, and Wahluna and Tlesca were lost forever.

In another version of the ancient story, the young Blackfoot chief, Tlesca, and the Nez Perce princess, Wahluna, escaped the monster's fury and reached the shore near the
Blackfoot camp. Ever afterward, the Nez Perce have been
apprehensive about venturing upon the waters of Wallowa
Lake, and the ancient enmity with the Blackfoot continued

The Nez Perce, Kutenai, Yakima, Sinkiuse, and other tribes of the Plateau had roving hunting habits much like those of the Plains tribes—and they hunted the bison in or near their homelands well into the eighteenth century. This is typical winter headgear with buffalo scalp and horns. WCHM by Joseph H. Wherry

until the white man's arrival and the consequent destruction of the bison herds beyond the Shining Mountains in Montana.

It is still dangerous, it is said, for cattle to graze too close to Wallowa Lake, but the monster crabs are believed to have disappeared.

Serpent Monsters of the Northwest

Lurking throughout the central part of the Pacific Northwest Coast were giant serpents, harbingers of everything that is evil. Some had a head at each end with enormous teeth and long tongues.

The Hai-et-lik of the Nootka country could shed his scales and become very slippery when attacked. Lightning flashed

Plateau horse gear was virtually like that
of the Plains by 1800. Squaw saddles
graced many of the tough Cayuse ponies
and Nez Perce Appaloosa horses; their warrior mates rode bareback. The hook on the
front pommel secured an infant's cradle
board to the mother's mount. Saddles were
made of bone and wood covered with raw-
hide. WCHM by Joseph H. Wherry

The late Chief Pete Wapato recalled seeing
the first whites come to Lake Chelan in
Washington when he was a small boy. This
photo of c.1929 shows the author as a boy,
when he spent many happy days with the
Chief hearing the old stories and fishing
with him on the mountain lake where a
monster is said to have lived. Joseph H.
Wherry

Lines at each side of the mouth with white
dots symbolize the tentacles and suckers of
Cuttlefish—the devilfish monster who destroyed the Tlingit salmon-drying camp.
In the winter ceremonies such a mask
would be worn by a participant acting the
part of the monster. TM by Joseph H.
Wherry

from the eyes in the Hai-et-lik's single head, and his likeness was carved on totemic house posts on the Olympic Peninsula in Washington, where the Quinault-Salish and the independent Quilliute are believed to have obtained the myth from the Makah. The latter lived near Cape Flattery and were the only Nootka tribe in the United States. Most terrible of all monsters in the region, however, was the two-headed Sisiutl, who roamed the lands of the Kwakiutl and Nootka on Vancouver Island. He was supernatural, impossible to kill without strong spirit power, and was four feet in diameter and seldom less than twenty feet long. Often in league with Thunderbird, who also made lightning and thunder with his eyes and wings, respectively, Sisiutls were at home either on land or in the sea. At each end of the body was a head, and in the middle was a human face proving supernatural soul power. Looking upon a Sisiutl could cause instant death. The creatures could escape by shrinking instantly into small size.

Even larger was the related two-headed Tsi-a-kish, who swallowed large canoes and whale hunters. One time an Indian encountered a monstrous Tsi-a-kish. Fortunately the man was a shaman and was immune to the lightning bolts because he had strong guardian spirits whose songs he knew. When the Indian sang his spirit songs, the Tsi-a-kish disintegrated and an entire tribe was released from captivity inside the monster.

The Monster Devilfish

Long ago there were devilfish so large that their tentacles could wrap around entire villages. The Tlingit of southeast Alaska were most troubled by these denizens of the deep, and they were careful to locate their salmon-drying racks so they could not be seen from the sea. One time, though, a Tlingit band was careless and built their drying racks in an exposed place. Sure enough, a monster was watching as the people hung their salmon to dry. When the sun shone on the fresh red meat, Devilfish was attracted by the brightness of the sight. Without warning Devilfish's tentacles lashed out, grasped the entire village, and dragged all of the houses and the people down into his sea cave.

Fortunately three brothers were away hunting. When they returned, they knew what had happened. "The devilfish has captured our village and all of our clan is gone," said the youngest brother.

"You must cut four spruce trees and make long spears of them," the oldest brother told the middle brother. "First, though, we must rest four days."

After four days the three brothers went out on the sea in their canoe, which they had loaded with large stones. As soon as they began throwing the stones into the water, Devilfish swam upward at the canoe and broke it. While the youngest brother swam for the shore, his two older brothers jumped on Devilfish and jabbed their spruce spears into its ugly body. As they fought the monster they sang spirit songs; thus they were able to kill the creature, which sank and carried them along down into the depths of the sea.

Younger brother, safe ashore, went to the next village where he had friends who gave him food and heard his words.

"We must go search for your brothers," the village chief said, and the youngest brother led the warriors to where his village had been. He also pointed to the place on the sea where his brothers had killed Devilfish.

"Your brothers are lost," his friends said after a search of the sea. "Now we must cut our hair short and have a feast for

Fine stylized engravings of fins beside the mouth mark this copper mask as symbolizing the mighty Sea Bear monster. Decorated with bear fur and abalone shell teeth and eyes, about 12 inches high, this is a Tlingit, Haida, or Tsimsyan mask, most probably the latter from the style. The wearer peeped through the tiny holes in the mask eyes. MPA by Joseph H. Wherry

the dead. No longer will Devilfish menace our villages."
After the death ceremonies, the younger brother went back to
live in the village of his clansmen.

This is what happened sometimes when devilfish grew
into monsters. This hasn't happened for many years and
probably will never happen again. Devilfish is on some totem
poles.

The Sea Bear

Have you ever wondered why some bears carved on headdresses and totem poles have a huge fin? There are very good
reasons, and here is how the custom began.

Many Tsimsyan hunters once went into the mountains up
the Skeena River to kill mountain goats. They killed too
many and the mountain goat spirits were enraged. Fleeing
down the mountains, the surviving hunters found refuge beside a lake where they fished for trout. One day an enormous
bear rose out of the lake and smashed the raft of the hunters.
In the battle the hunters killed the great bear. Then they recognized the monster as the supernatural Sea Bear because it
had three human faces on its tall fin and long human hair on
its head. In an act of great folly the hunters tore the claws
from Sea Bear's feet, cut its hair, and—worst of all—cut off
the monster's head!

In a furious rage at such rash acts, the water spirits caused
foam to rise on the lake and high up the sides of the mountains to avenge the slaughter of the mountain goat people and
the supernatural Sea Bear.

"We must throw away the claws and hair," shouted the
chief of the hunters, "or we will be destroyed." When the

143

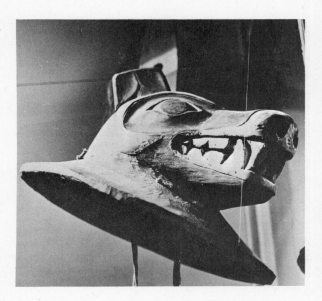

Carved, broad-brimmed wood hats topped with totemic crests and mythical creatures were as important when greeting guests and on formal occasions as were masks on the Northwest Coast. Once the property of the Tlingit Chief Shakes near Wrangel, this hat is decorated with either the supernatural Grizzly Bear of the Sea or the sea wolf Wasgo. DAM by Joseph H. Wherry

hunters had done this, the foam receded and the lake was calm; the spirits were assuaged.

Hurrying home to their village, the hunters displayed the head of the monster. A special song was composed and a feast was given. Ever since then the supernatural Sea Bear has been highly regarded and shamans invoke its spirit, because when properly treated, the being's power is very beneficial.

* * *

There were other monsters in the beginning but these are the ones everyone learns about.

This is all.

144

The Mystical Way
of Life

s already observed, the Indians were, simultaneously, realists and mystics. Realities and mysteries of life were understandable through contemplation, dreams, visions, and rituals. Imagination played an important part in the daily walk through a life which was one with the supernatural powers of nature! For every beneficial or evil experience there was a supernatural reason. For every undertaking, the spirits were invoked. Here are some of the mythological traditions which have survived.

How Death Began

Throughout much of the West Coyote is blamed for bringing Death to the world. In fact the howling of Coyote in the stillness of the night is evidence of the dastardly deed perpetuated ages ago before his ancestor was exiled. This is how

The sturdiest houses outside of the Southwest region were built of huge, rough-hewn planks by the tribes of the Northwest Coast. This scale model is of a northwestern California redwood house of the type favored by the Yurok, Tolowa, Hupa, and Karok. Note the flat roof section between the side slopes. From the Columbia River delta through Tlingit country, cedar was used with a double pitched roof. CSIM by Joseph H. Wherry

the Wintun, Chimariko, and others of northern California tell what happened when all creatures lived forever.

Coyote conceived his nefarious scheme during a long winter when famine threatened. "There are so many people," he howled, "that there is not enough food." He ran everywhere screaming, "Death must be allowed to take away the old ones."

Coyote's suggestion was scandalous and the shaman was very angry. "This is the worst idea old Coyote has ever had. Nevertheless, it is true that there is not enough food for everyone. I will call a council at the sacred place."

When all of the people—including all of the animals—were assembled, the shaman addressed them.

"Coyote says that if there were fewer people there would be no starvation. Coyote says we should allow Death to walk during the night. What do you all think of the idea?"

Many said that Coyote was up to another of his tricks and that he meant to harm them. Finally Coyote shouted, "Those who die will be able to come back to us later. I mean no harm."

"What do you propose to do, then?" the shaman asked. "Speak, Coyote."

"We must cut a hole in the sky," Coyote replied with a sly look. "Then the people can come back when there is plenty of food for all to eat."

"But how can we make a hole in the sky when there is no rock, no tree, no mountain high enough to reach the sky?" someone asked.

"Oh, I know how this can be done," old Coyote replied. "It is quite simple."

"You must tell us how," said the shaman who was the wisest of men.

"The best warrior will shoot an arrow into the sky. The arrow will hold fast and then other arrows will be shot and

The world view of the Plateau tribes in British Columbia and Alberta. Toward the West was the "Land of the Dead," usually over a mountain or through a pass—a view consistent with that of many other Plateau and northern California tribes.

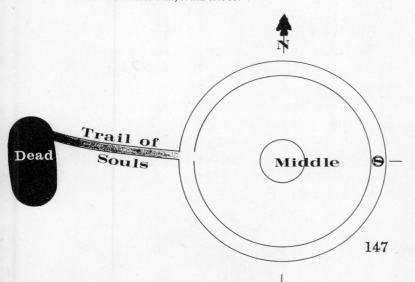

147

Yurok white deerskin dancer wears sea-lion-tusk headdress and buckskin kilt.
Sketch by L. D. Sutton

earth and sky will be connected with a chain of arrows," said Coyote. "Then those old people who die can climb up to the place of the dead. Later they can return on the arrow path."

The wise shaman was suspicious of Coyote, but he thought the idea was quite good. All of the people agreed because they were hungry.

"All right," the shaman agreed. "Bring your bows and arrows to the sacred rock."

When the warriors were assembled, the shaman told the strongest marksman to shoot at the sky. "See!" yelped Coyote as the arrow flew straight and true to the sky where it stuck, "I told you this would work."

148

By this time, however, all the people were so busy watching the warriors shoot arrow after arrow that they didn't notice Coyote laughing to himself. That old scamp chuckled every time an arrow flew skyward where it stuck to the previous arrow. After a time the chain of arrows reached from the sky to the top of the sacred rock where the last arrow was secured. As darkness came, the shaman spoke again as he stood by the base of the great boulder.

"Here there is a secret entrance which I will open to allow Death to enter while we sleep. Those whom Death chooses will go through this door and climb to the sky on the chain of arrows."

When the shaman had spoken, all of the people went to their houses.

"Who will Death choose tonight?" they asked each other. "There are many old ones who can work no longer."

During the night a very old warrior died as he slept, as did an eagle who was so weak he could no longer fly and several others. The dead people followed Death to the sacred rock. After entering, they climbed to the land of the dead in the sky at the end of the chain of arrows.

"What shall we do?" the sorrowing survivors asked the shaman the next day. "We have more to eat but we are lonely for our loved ones."

Every night more old people died and went away. Finally the shaman said, "Our loved ones will return when the stars come close."

"But where is Coyote?" someone asked.

"He is in his den," said another.

"What is that evil one doing and why does he not associate with us?" a widow asked. "This trouble is all Coyote's fault. We never should have listened to him!"

One night while everyone else slept, Coyote slunk from his cave and climbed to the top of the sacred place—the big rock.

In late autumn the timbered hills along the Klamath River in Yurok country are misty. Souls went westward over these sacred hills to the Land of the Dead. Joseph H. Wherry

Grabbing hold of the last arrow, he pulled all of the arrows out of the sky. Down they came with a crash on top of Coyote, and all the people came rushing to the holy place.

"See what Coyote has done," the people cried. "Now our loved ones can never return from the land of the dead."

"You have performed your most evil deed," the shaman scolded Coyote. "From this time forth you must leave the company of people. Because you have tricked us, because you have brought Death to us and have destroyed the path by which the dead could return, you will be hunted by men."

Ever since that time Coyote has been lonely and has howled at night with his nose pointed toward the sky where the chain of arrows connected the heavens and the earth.

This unhappy state of affairs came about differently in Pomo country when Coyote saw a rattlesnake go into a hole

150

one day. Dancing around the hole, Coyote called all of the people to come and observe.

"A beautiful bird is hiding in the hole," Coyote said. "If you want to see the bird, you must dance as I do."

The chief's daughter danced close to the hole and the rattlesnake struck her on the ankle. When the maiden cried out in pain, Coyote growled, "Your dancing is all wrong."

In a few hours the maiden died from the venom. "Coyote," said the grieving chief, "my daughter must live again."

This is how Coyote had planned to bring Death to the world. "No," he said, "if people always live forever, there will be too many people and not enough acorns and other food."

"You, Coyote, are to blame for my daughter's death," the chief retorted. Secretly he plotted revenge. When the dead maiden was dressed in her finest clothes, she was cremated with much ceremony.

Several days later Coyote's lovely daughter died. The chief had had her poisoned. Now it was the trickster Coyote's turn to mourn and he howled all night. The next day he came to the chief.

"My daughter must live again," Coyote cried. "Let it be so."

"No," said the angry chief. "When my daughter died because of your mischief, you said it was best to let dead people remain dead to prevent the world having too many people."

"Yes, you are right," admitted Coyote. "We must dress my daughter and cremate her as we did your daughter."

The people had another funeral pyre and Coyote mourned and howled every night. It is for this reason that Death came to the world and that Coyote always howls.

* * *

Coyote brought death to the Southwest too. According to the Apache, Coyote decreed death if a stone, which he threw into a stream, sank to the bottom.

In the lower Colorado River country and particularly among the Mojave Indians, the creating deity, Matavilye, also ordained death to prevent overpopulation. Matavilye became ill after many busy years and he died intentionally—with overtones of suicide—to set an example. The Mojave were obsessed with the idea that any prolonged activity of one kind would bring on mental illness and insanity. Hence many Mojave still prefer frequent changes in occupation.

The origin of death—or the justification for mortality—has occasioned fewer myths on the Northwest Coast than elsewhere. Tsimsyan tradition holds that Elderberry Bush's children were born before those of Stone. Consequently humans are mortal like Elderberry, while Stone is immortal. In the Southwest the Navajo creation story—told previously—incorporates the origin of death and is typical for the region.

Exquisitely carved forehead plates, worn by Tsimsyan chiefs during ceremonies, displayed totemic clan crests. Top down: large figure appears to be Beaver surrounded by eight frog children and probably refers to upper Skeena River chief's daughter who became wife of the frog chief and founded the frog clan (NMC); large hawk crest with five men (PMBC); eagle or hawk with thirteen men (PMBC). These were worn with robes of ermine, sea otter, and other luxurious pelts. The Tlingit of southeast Alaska carved similar devices. Joseph H. Wherry

The Land of the Dead

On the southwestern fringe of the Plateau region the divinities were rather vaguely defined; supernaturals were taken for granted with little in the way of explanation. Kumookumts was the great culture hero of the Modocs of northeastern California; he was also known to the neighboring Klamath. The creator of people, he ordained death and the reason was fear of too many people.

One day Kumookumts decided to visit his daughter who had died. In the land of the dead he observed that all the people were searching for swan eggs, which they placed in burden baskets. Selecting a basket, Kumookumts was unable to keep the eggs from falling through the hole in the bottom until someone told him to stuff the hole with tule. When he returned to his camp, however, his basket was empty, and though it was time for darkness, daylight was everywhere. This was because everything in the land of the dead was the opposite of conditions in the land of the living: day was dark, night was light, full was empty, and so on.

Next Kumookumts determined to gather the bones of his daughter and other relatives who were dead. With his basket full of bones, he began the long walk home across the mountain bordering the land of the dead. Before reaching the summit, Kumookumts felt something pinch him and he itched terribly. When he put his basket down to scratch, all of the bones fell out and rolled back down the mountainside. Three or four more times he collected the bones, and each time he felt the same mysterious pinching. The spirits of the dead were pinching him. Kumookumts finally decided the dead should stay at rest and so he advised the Modoc and the surrounding tribes. Thus, it is so.

Pugnacious and aggressive appearance of this black-and-red mask, once owned by a Bella Coola shaman, characterized the power of his spirits who assisted him in curing the sick and restoring lost souls.
MPM by Joseph H. Wherry

When Tribes and Clans Were Formed

The Navajo myth of the emergence of people upon the earth, already told, is related to the traditions extant among the Pueblo Indians. Close proximity during the last thousand years or more has produced mythological similarities despite linguistic differences.

As with all primitive peoples, the center of their own particular culture also was—at least to them—the center of the world. To the Keresan Indians, their emergence place, "Shipap," is also the place where people go after death; this place is believed to be near Cochiti pueblo. (It will be remembered that the Navajo place of emergence, a marsh in the Grand Junction, Colorado area, is also the entry to that na-

155

This unidentified, somewhat jolly-looking supernatural bird mask with human hair could be of Bella Coola or Kwakiutl origin, with the odds favoring the latter. Smooth surfaces were ingeniously accomplished by using sharkskin as we employ sandpaper.
DAM by Joseph H. Wherry

tion's place of the dead.) But we must return to primal times when all of the people on earth, according to Pueblo tradition, were residing communally at White House. Here there was peace and the two sacred mothers, Naotsiti and Uretsiti, managed their matriarchies most amicably; they were sisters.

When the population expanded, however, the people left White House and disputes, inevitably occurred between the two mothers. Each of them presumed the prerogatives of

156

leadership. One day Naotsiti, who was the Navajo mother, demanded a test to determine whether she or Uretsiti, the Cochiti mother, was the greatest. With all of the people as witnesses, the two mothers stood, side by side, facing the East at sunrise.

"The winner will be the one on whom Sun first shines," Naotsiti declared. Uretsiti agreed.

As the Sun rose over the eastern horizon, his rays first shone on Uretsiti, the shorter of the two. Her height had caused Naotsiti to become conceited, and thus she was shocked when she found herself still partially shaded while Uretsiti was completely bathed in the rays of the Sun.

"You are the winner," Naotsiti said to Uretsiti, "but after four days we shall have another trial."

At the appointed time the two feuding sisters called the people together again. After scattering corn meal to the four directions, Naotsiti hit Uretsiti. Though knocked down, Uretsiti got up quickly and struck Naotsiti to the ground, where they struggled until Uretsiti conquered the taller sister, who immediately turned into a woodrat and escaped among the rocks.

In some versions, the weapon used was a throwing stick of the type used in hunting rabbits. Both mothers went their separate ways after the duel. This event established the Navajo taboo against killing woodrats out of respect to their primal mother. Many of the Pueblo people believe that Naotsiti was the mother of all the world's people except the Pueblo Indians. The latter revere Uretsiti and call her "our Mother." In a remote cave on the Rio Grande there is a shrine to "our Mother" where offerings are brought on ceremonial occasions.

* * *

157

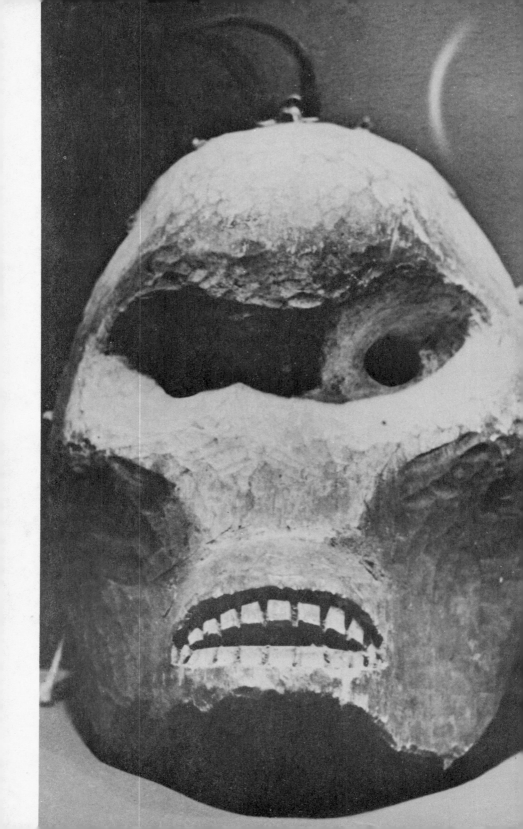

According to Navajo mythology, however, their clans came from virtually everywhere to the lands encompassed by the Four Sacred Mountains. Much of New Mexico and Arizona, and even lands outside this area, may be considered in Navajo tradition. After the monsters were destroyed in the primal times, the first clan, the Tall House People, were created in Chaco Canyon by the gods whom we shall meet in the next chapter. These were pueblo village dwellers who cultivated corn. Other clans probably came from Apache, Yuman, Pueblo, and others. Inspiration for most of the ceremonial costumes of the Navajo derived from close proximity to the Pueblo tribes. The Navajo have been wonderfully detailed in Ruth Underhill's *The Navajos*, a book recommended to the reader intent upon further study about this great tribe.

Throughout much of the Basin and Plateau regions and in California the origin of the many tribal groups tallies generally with the Pomo story of the simultaneous creation of people and tribes by Coyote assisted by Lizard who was proud of his five fingers. This myth was related earlier.

In southern California, however, Mastamho (a god shared by neighboring Shoshoni, Diegueño, Mojave, and Yuma tribes) turned all of the first people into animals. After this act Mastamho took clay and made ten very small ancestors of each of the present tribes in the area. Quickly growing to normal human size, these new people procreated and became tribes near a mountain somewhere north of Blythe on the California side of the Colorado River. A totemic belief in animal

A few locks of human hair top this "Speaker of the Ghost" mask used by Kwakiutl shamans in winter spirit ceremonies. Collected by George Hunt c.1900. AMNH by Joseph H. Wherry

ancestors—wildcat, coyote, etc.—is similar to the very sophisticated totemism of the Northwest Coast, where animal
ancestors and mythical supernatural experiences with animals, evolved into a complicated system of jealously guarded
family and clan crests which reached their zenith on the elaborately carved totem poles and masks. The "Out of the Foam
from Asia" myth in Chapter Three relates to an Eagle clan of
the Tsimsyan. Raven, Wolf, Bear, and Frog were other popular totemic clan symbols on the Northwest Coast.

One day the lovely daughter of a Tlingit chief was gathering berries with several of her high-caste friends. On the way
home the princess stumbled and fell as the group crossed the
trail of a bear. All would have gone well, but the chief's
daughter made insulting remarks about bears. This was a
grievous error, as she well knew, because animal spirits always heard what was said about them. From that moment
bad fortune stalked her. When her basket broke, her friends
went on ahead. Darkness came and with it the sound of foot-
steps in an otherwise silent forest. Suddenly a young man appeared beside her. When he picked up her broken basket, she
followed him. Happy for his company, she was nevertheless
frightened, for he was a stranger. Presently they came to a
village she had never seen.

"We will go to my father's house," the young man said.
"My father is the chief here."

All her life the princess had longed for the day when she
would meet just the right young man—the son of a great
chief, of course.

"I have found a wife," the young man announced as they
entered the great house.

After a huge feast, the newlyweds lived in one of the apart-
ments in the chef's house. After a few weeks, though, the

Indians of the Northwest Coast made durable wooden boxes and decorated them with carved totemic clan crests. The small 6-inch-high Tlingit box (USNM) *held trinkets, while the large Haida box* (PMBC) *with beaver crest was a child's mortuary coffin. Similar large food and cooking boxes were waterproofed with bear grease or fat of other animals.* Joseph H. Wherry

princess became uneasy at the many mysterious happenings. When wet garments were shaken over the fire, the flames sparkled and leaped higher with phosphorescent lights. When she accompanied her husband on a fishing trip, she observed the other women gathering the wettest wood they could find. Curiously this wet wood made the hottest fires; the dry wood she gathered did not burn well at all. Ashamed of her inability to do the work expected of her, the young woman became very homesick for her own people.

So it went for three years, during which time the lost princess gave birth to two boys. Aroused by a strange noise one night, she was startled to see a huge bear beside her. Then she realized that she was in the village of the bear people and that her husband was the son of the bear chief. Now the flashing phosphorescent flames from wet wood and drops of water were understandable. Touching the great shaggy bear beside her, it grunted and miraculously changed into its human form. She had been taken as a bride by the prince of the bears.

"The bear spirits heard me insult them that day so long ago," she said to herself as she thought back to the time she met her husband. "This place only looks like a house; it is really the den of the bears and they have bewitched me."

The next day her husband sharpened his weapons—or so it appeared. In reality, he was grinding his teeth as if to prepare for battle. "Could my brothers be searching for me?" the princess asked herself. Hearing a dog bark, the princess rushed to the door. Sure enough, she recognized her brothers approaching.

"My brothers are coming," she said to her husband. "They are your brothers-in-law. Please do not harm them."

Stepping outside, she called, "Do not kill my husband!" But it was too late to prevent tragedy. As the bear prince came out, her brothers loosed a volley of arrows. All of them struck the bear prince. He fell dead at his wife's feet.

"My brothers, please do not cut my husband up for meat," the long-lost princess pleaded. "We must bury him here. Then I will come home with you to our father."

From a shaman's grave house at Yakutat, where it was collected before 1887 by George Emmons, this figure is carved with wolf (on chest) and bear (on knees) guardian spirits. About 24 inches tall, it is decorated with shell teeth and human hair. Black, blue, brown, and red are used.
AMNH by Joseph H. Wherry

Bear masks were employed to illustrate Bear Mother myths, to display family crests, or to portray one's guardian spirit in the winter dances. Women protégés of Bear's spirit were industrious housekeepers and good mothers, while Bear gave men great endurance and made them good hunters. This Kwakiutl mask is from Quatsino Sound on Vancouver Island. DAM by Joseph H. Wherry

For the first time she realized that her appearance must have startled her brothers. No longer was the spirit power of the bear upon her. She was a Tlingit princess again, but her fine clothes were ragged.

"Come," her brothers said, "bring your children; we must be on our way before the other bears return."

Back home again the princess found new happiness while her sons became great warriors and founders of the Kats lineage, a name much respected among the Tlingit. This is how Bear became a valuable crest ages before the arrival of the Europeans. Bear masks were popular all along the Northwest Coast and the many Bear Mother myths are all closely related.

*   *   *

Another version tells how the chief's daughter discovered who her captors were. Escaping from them, she came to a lake where there was a huge canoe which was wearing a decorated hat. Even stranger, the canoe beckoned to her to climb aboard. Soon the supernatural canoe was flying toward the Sun, which it entered. When the sons of the Sun saw the princess, they loved her and she became their wife.

After a time the princess had a baby boy. One day when the Sun was over her father's village, her husbands loaded the great canoe with presents of food and grease for their father-in-law. On the way to the village the canoe—which was really an enormous grizzly bear—would stop frequently and the husbands would feed it grease from one of the food boxes. On arrival at her father's house, the princess was greeted by her brothers and her mother, who had given her up for dead. Although her husbands were in the canoe, they appeared as rays of copper-colored sunlight to all but the long-lost daughter.

At the homecoming feast her sunlight husbands decided they would leave her, and though the princess pursued them and caught them, they slipped from her grasp and deserted her and her baby. When the boy grew up, his mother made him arrows and a fine bow. One day he returned from the sea very frightened—a monster with a huge red mouth had come out of the water toward him. His mother explained that the being was his father's canoe, that it would not harm him, and that he should shoot an arrow into its mouth. When the young man returned to the shore, the being came toward him again and he shot an arrow into its gaping mouth. The arrow caused the canoe, which was made of copper, to shatter.

After many trips to his mother's house, the young man had gathered all of the shining copper, which he used in making knives and spear points, the first metal objects his

Used in Increase and Bladder ceremonies by Bering Sea coast Eskimos but not identifiable as to creature symbolized, this mask is 17 inches long. One leg and a flipper appear to be missing. This might be a female shaman's mask—lower face has chintatoo marks—and the creature could represent Whale's spirit. University of Alaska Museum

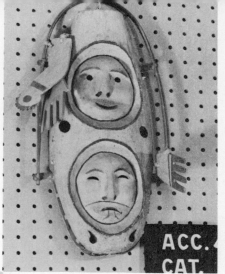

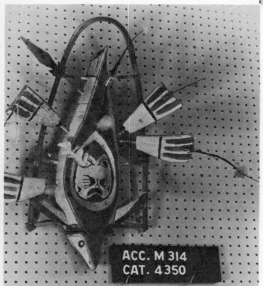

Made somewhere along the Bering Sea coast and apparently quite old, this is a Salmon tornait mask used in shamanistic rituals invoking Sedna and her sea spirits in the Bladder festivals. About 29 inches long, the fins are stylized, but the symbol at top left is not known. University of Alaska Museum

Eskimo craftsmen made a variety of eyeshades and slotted snow goggles long before they ever saw a white man, but the black design around the eyes is probably a stylized outline. Unidentified as to Alaska source or collection date, this mask, with little doubt, represents a supernatural half-man-half-animal spirit—some sort of fish, possibly halibut. The arms and legs complete the human half-form, the inua or thinking part of which is represented by the well-detailed face. WCHM by Joseph H. Wherry

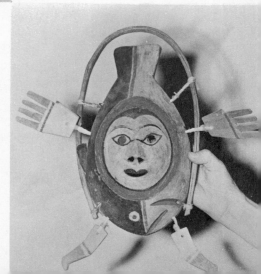

mother's people had ever seen. He even made a house out of copper plates which he fashioned by pounding. The young prince made the first "coppers"—the large shield-shaped devices which came to have great value.

When the young man married the daughter of an important chief and took her to his copper house, all the people became very curious. To pay for his new wife, the Sun's grandson gave his father-in-law many fine "coppers," and this is how their value was established long ago. With his great copper wealth, the young man—actually a prince in his own right—gave many potlatches and became a great chief. From Yakutat to Vancouver Island the value of "coppers" became well known. Raw copper found in outcroppings of rocks was pounded into knives and other objects and was used to trim many ceremonial masks like those illustrated.

Rebuilding the World

All of the Indians were aware of the annual birth and growing cycles of animals and plants, the trees from which they obtained acorns and nuts, the fish in the rivers. Among the Eskimos, the Bladder Festival assures a plentiful supply of walrus and seal the next year. During this ceremony, the bladders—in which the animals' souls reside—are displayed. Near the end of the festival the bladders are put back in the sea to be reincarnated. Similarly, one of the most important ceremonies was that of the first salmon in the many parts of the West where this succulent fish was a staple food. During the long winters when the rivers of the far Northwest Coast were choked with ice, the people lived off their stocks of dried

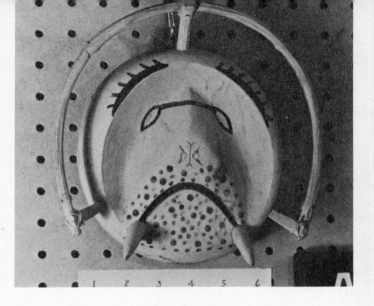

*An old-style walrus spirit mask, this ex-
ample was collected on Nunivak Island in
1927. The white face has red and black
eyes and eyebrow details with blue and red
spots around the mouth. The ceremonial
use is unknown.* Univerity of Alaska Museum

and smoked salmon. This was true of the Tlingit, Haida,
Tsimsyan and many tribes farther south, as well as inland in
the Plateau Region. Many times starvation threatened when
the salmon stocks dwindled before the ice broke up and the
salmon began their annual migration to the spawning
grounds in the gravel-bottomed rivers. The season's first salmon was awaited eagerly.

One time the son of a respected woman took a piece of salmon from the food box without permission. After being
scolded, the boy went far up the Skeena River, where he sat
down and sulked. Presently he heard the sound of a canoe,
and a voice called to him. Hurrying in the direction of the
shout, he came to a big canoe.

"Get in," someone said, and in he climbed. The canoe went

168

farther up the river and came to a village with large houses. The front of the first house was painted with the "Qanis," or dog salmon design. (This term is applied in the North Pacific to any male salmon which is migrating to the spawning place. There is also a salmon species called by this name which is smaller than the quinnat, or king almon, and has no spots on its fins.) Other fine housefronts were painted with the coho, sockeye, steelhead, and spring salmon. In front of the spring salmon house the mysterious canoe ran ashore and the canoe people entered. The boy followed them.

"You are in the house of the salmon people," a girl said. "You healed the crippled leg of the salmon chief when you took the fish from your mother's salmon box. The chief's leg was cured because you straightened the salmon."

Of course the young man was baffled at what the girl—

Collected on the lower Kuskokwim River c.1920, this Eskimo walrus mask has a black head with the mouth and eyes outlined in red. A dancer held the mask by clamping his teeth on an inside projection and looked through the mouth past the tusks. Fairly compact, it is 6 inches across with wood-peg whiskers. It must be quite old, as it has been broken and repaired with sinew or leather lashings. It was probably used in Increase and Bladder festivals. University of Alaska Museum

169

who was really Mouse Woman in human form—told him. "The chief had you brought here so he can reward you properly. However," she cautioned, "eat none of the food they offer you, not even what looks like berries, because they will be the eyes of dead people!"

"But I am hungry," the boy complained, "what shall I eat?"

"Wait until tomorrow," Mouse Woman instructed. "Then go outside where many children, who are really salmon, will be playing. Catch a child, hit him with your club, and eat him. Then you must carefully burn every bone and all the salmon parts you do not eat."

Doing as he was instructed, the young man discovered that the child became a real salmon the instant it was clubbed. Satisfying his hunger, the boy burned the bones and returned to the fine house. Suddenly the children burst through the door, one of them screaming, "One of my eyes is gone."

Instantly Mouse Woman materialized. "You failed to burn one of the eyes of the salmon," she whispered. "Go find the eye and burn it. Hurry!"

When he had completed his task, the young man saw that the child's eyes were normal again. Several days later the salmon chief sent a nephew to determine whether the new leaves were on the trees. The seeds were their food.

"No, Uncle," the youth said when he returned. "The new leaves are not yet sprouted."

A few weeks later a second nephew was sent on the same errand. "Far up the river the new leaves have budded," he reported.

"That is good," the chief said. "We will go to the seed grounds tomorrow."

A salmon skin was given to the houseguest from down the Skeena. "Put this on for our journey," the chief ordered. "You will go with us."

170

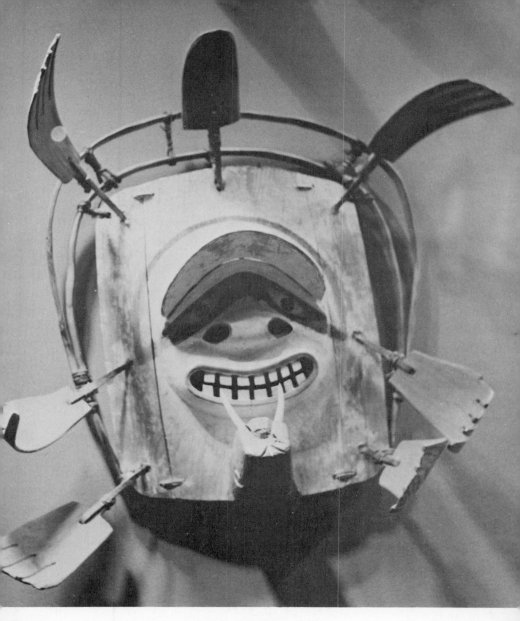

Collected, date unknown, by the Alaska Commercial Company probably somewhere along the Bering Sea or Bristol Bay coast, this large mask probably represents one or more sea spirits. Perhaps the inverted walrus at bottom was the tutelary spirit of a shaman who officiated at the Bladder festivals when Sedna and her tornaits were invoked to assure a renewal and increase of sea animals. Black was used for the mouth and around the right eye. The left-eye shading, the flippers, the single paddle at top, and the walrus and baleen hoops are deep red. RLMA by Joseph H. Wherry

*Omnipresent throughout the Eskimo world
were half-man-half-animal spirits whose
mask representations were employed by
male and female shamans. Such masks usually had encircling loops of baleen to which
were attached arms and legs to complete
the human half of the spirit. Common folk
had less ornate masks like this, which portrayed the likeness of a sea otter in black.*
University of Alaska Museum

Diving into the water, the young man discovered the
salmon skin enabled him to swim as fast as the salmon
people. In fact the young man became a salmon, and with the
others he swam upstream toward the spawning grounds.

"See what a huge Qanis I have caught," shouted a chief
who was netting salmon in the rapids near his village. "This
is the largest salmon I have ever seen." And the chief called a
servant and ordered him to take the big dog salmon to his
wife.

172

When the chief's wife cut the great Qanis open with her clamshell knife to prepare it for a feast, she discovered a child in the fish.

From this experience with the supernatural salmon, the people learned to ceremonially burn all of the bones and un-eaten parts of the first salmon caught in the spring. By this means the salmon spirits knew that their clan was respected and the ceremony assured that the salmon would be plentiful. Thus the first-salmon ceremony became a great event and evolved into a sort of "new year" ritual in which all of the nature spirits were invoked to assure that all things—the world in effect—would be renewed.

Even the Plateau tribes far inland honored the first salmon taken from rivers like the Columbia and the Snake and their many tributaries. The Northern Shoshoni, the Bannock, the Yakima, the Nez Perce, the Okanogan, and others prepared great feasts at which the first salmon was held up to the sun. Sometimes a chief or shaman would hold the ceremonial fish to each of the four directions as he invoked the continued blessings of the Great Oversoul, the Sky Chief. Then the first salmon would be passed to all present—or the tribesmen would file past the fish, which sometimes was displayed as if on an altar—and each person would break off one small bite. After this solemn ritual—a primitive sacramental meal which should have been understandable to the first white Christian pioneers—general feasting would take place in a spirit of thanksgiving for the bounties produced by the Sun Father and Mother Earth.

The bones of the first salmon were either burned as on the far Northwest Coast, buried with further invocations, or sol-emnly returned to the stream where the salmon had been caught. Free again, the bones were believed to find their way

173

Another half-man-half-animal spirit mask with forehead and nose painted blue; the top rim is red; the mink or otter is blue. Such a mask signified the owner had been spirited away to the Land of Dead or for instruction by one of these supernaturals who evidenced his presence by thundering and stamping noises. Sometimes carved with an animal body having a human face, these were friendly spirits who smilingly bestowed good health and fortune upon the person who was stolen away temporarily. Such male spirits were called excit; females were called yeyehuk. University of Alaska Museum

back to the village of the salmon people, where the first salmon would become whole again, thus assuring a plentiful supply the next year when the renewal ceremony would be celebrated in a never-ending life cycle.

Similar spring ceremonies occurred on the Washington, Oregon and California coasts, where the first salmon, berries, and acorns were celebrated in a similar manner reminiscent of the first-fruits rituals of the Old World.

* * *

174

In the areas drained by the Klamath, Trinity, and Rogue rivers many of the tribes—the Yurok, Hupa, Karok, Chetco, Umpqua, etc.—also had a deerskin dance.

A sickness of fever was killing the Indians in southwestern Oregon. No one can remember just when this happened, but it was a long, long time ago. Some of the Indians went high into the coast range. When a chief's daughter took sick, the people were very distressed and were certain that all of them would die. Some of the ancient stories say that the princess was of the Umpqua. When the crisis was upon her, the women of the chief's house surrounded her bed, and as they chanted the men sat cross-legged outside. As she was dying, a white deer came into the camp clearing from the forest. Gracefully the white deer walked around the shelter several times, then entered the doorway without fear of the people and came to the maiden. After a moment the white deer touched its mouth to the dying maiden's lips. Ceasing the death chant, the women watched as the white deer turned and walked out of the shelter as silently as it had arrived and crossed the clearing to the forest, where it disappeared. Instantly the searing fever broke and the chief's daughter stood up completely cured. Naturally the miracle was reported far and wide.

Throughout a vast area to this day, the white deer is still regarded by some as the supernatural healing representative of the Supreme Being. A few white or albino deer have been known to exist in historic times. Among some tribes, the Yurok, Hupa, and Karok for example, it is taboo to kill a white deer for sport, but some white deerskins have been treasured for untold years. Some say these are bleached hides of normal deer. At the White Deerskin Dance, held in the early autumn and rarely in recent years, the sacred skins are held aloft by a line of devotees (as shown herewith in the sketch of a single dancer) who dance in place to the accompaniment of singers and drummers.

175

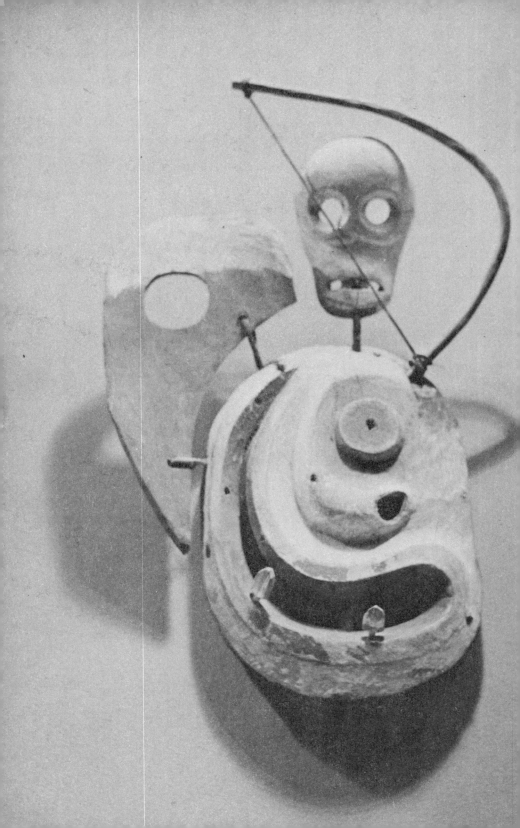

In front of the dancers other celebrants display the highly valued strings of dentalium and heavy obsidian blades. The latter, of red, white, or black obsidian, are the California equivalent of the "coppers" of the far Northwest Coast. Instead of masks, the participants wear a headpiece of sea-lion tusks. (According to an Indian friend and informant, however, a few masks were used at a Karok village near the present site of Orleans on the Klamath River, where the culture was a virtual carbon copy of that of the Yurok.) The sacred white deerskins are never sold; they remain family property from generation to generation and symbolize immortality, healing, and the assurance that the cycle of life depends upon a spiritual "rebuilding of the world." White skins were worth around $500 many years ago.

Despite efforts to eradicate the ancient mystical way of life, many Indians of the West still revere "the old ways." When strength-symbolizing eagle feathers can no longer be obtained, turkey feathers often are substituted for dance costumes. Recently after an annual feast—which now takes

A variant of the half-man-half-animal spirit theme, this Eskimo mask was collected around 1898 by Sheldon Jackson, the first Federal education representative in Alaska Territory. The darker portions are stained a deep red with traces of yellow around the mouth and protruding single eye, in which there is a small peephole. Concentric with the lopsided, grinning mouth is an animal-spirit symbol. The head above is secured by a baleen peg and could represent the mask owner who was spirited away by the half-man. The bow is strung with seal sinew. Considering the flipper on the side, the shaman owner probably used this mask when invoking Sedna before hunting whale and other sea animals. RLMA by Joseph H. Wherry

place on the Fourth of July—a fire was built in a circular "brush house" after sunset. To the drumming and chanting of their elders, several young men and boys danced. On their bodies were turkey feathers—the best possible under the circumstances. On their heads, however, were the traditional red-and-black flicker-feather headbands, and in their mouths they held reed whistles, in the manner of their ancestors. The place is called Kashia by the white people's Bureau of Indian Affairs—to the handful of Pomo in attendance, it is a pitiful, dry little forty-acre reservation called Tsunúnu Shinal, the "place of huckleberries." White trees, sacred albino redwoods, grow nearby in secret places.

The mystical way of life, the ceremonies which came in dreams and visions, has meaning to many Indians who still invoke the supernatural spirits as their ancestors did in their annual gatherings when they, and all of nature, are renewed by the Indian way which whites fail to comprehend.

The High Deities—
Creators and Protectors

 deity throughout much of North America was the sun. In the lower Mississippi Valley the sun was of major importance in ceremonial activity, and a cult of worship developed around that "life giver." On the plains individuals and tribes invoked Sun's blessings upon the hunt and in war. In the famous Sun Dance, warriors danced around a pole to which they were connected by rawhide thongs skewered through their own flesh, or they dragged heavy buffalo skulls by the thongs in a test of endurance and indifference to pain. The Sun Dance invaded the subject area with the Northern Shoshoni, and it is possible that some of the easternmost of the Southwest Indians came in contact with the Kiowa practice during occasional expeditions to the southern buffalo plains. Participants faced the sun for many hours, often an entire day, while invoking the blessings of the glowing center of our universe.

Probably nowhere in the West, however, was Sun the object of worship except among the Northern Shoshoni and

Bannock who offered prayers to it over the first salmon, as mentioned in the previous chapter. In such circumstances Sun approached the status of a supreme being, although formalized worship of that sort was rare indeed. Our old friend Coyote, who was creator, trickster, and culture hero over a vast area, was not a supreme being. Where there was a belief in one supreme being, it was generally vague, and terms interpreted loosely as Great Oversoul, He Who Dwells Above, Great Spirit, Sky Chief, and the like sufficed to identify him.

Major deities generally evolved out of the incorporation of central mythological characters into a body of ritualistic practices by medicine men or shamans. Actual religious practices are the subject of the next chapter. Here our concern is with the leading supernatural personality of each of the five major native religious cults in the West. These supernaturals cannot be equated precisely with a supreme being, but they were dominant in the religious life of the natives.

Our attention is first drawn to the Arctic, where there was almost no binding social organization or tribal authority, and where fear of the spirits of the unknown displaced any tendency toward worship as we understand the word.

The Eskimo Deity of the Sea

To the Eskimos across the roof of Canada and eastward she is called Sedna; to the Eskimos of Alaska she is usually referred to as the Old Woman, who inhabits the ocean and provides the seals, walruses, whales, and other sea creatures upon which life depends. For simplification, we'll call her Sedna.

A widower lived in a village on the shore with his daughter, Sedna, who was beautiful and sought after by all the young men in the area. Sedna, however, honored the suit of none until Fulmar flew overhead one day in spring as the ice was breaking up.

"Come with me to the land of birds," Fulmar sang. "Come with me where there is no hunger to my beautiful skin tent, where you shall have the finest furs to rest upon. All of my kinsmen will bring you whatever you wish and you will have feathers to wear, oil in your lamp, and plenty of meat to eat."

The song of Fulmar turned the lovely girl's head, and she went away with him. Sedna's pride was such that Fulmar's love song impressed her where all of the blandishments of the young men among her own people had failed. In Fulmar's house, Sedna was bitterly disappointed. Instead of being covered with fine skins, the hut was made of shabby fish skins, and her bed was a pile of uncomfortable walrus hides rather than the soft furs she had been promised. Her lamp contained no oil. There was nothing to eat except old dead fish (a fulmar is a scavenger species of the petrel family, which looks much like a herring gull and migrates as far south as the California coast). In short, the poor, proud maiden was cold, hungry, and homesick.

In her anguish Sedna sang to her father's spirit, hoping he would rescue her and take her home to her village where she was loved. When the next spring arrived, Sedna's father put to sea to visit her, and when he arrived he killed the deceitful Fulmar. With his daughter beside him in his skin boat, the father put to sea again. But the rescue was foredoomed to failure, and when the kinsmen of Fulmar returned to his tent and found the mangled body, they set out to find the fleeing wife and whoever had killed Fulmar. Crying their mournful sound—the same sound all fulmars still utter—the fulmars spied the boat on the sea, which they whipped into a terrible storm. Obviously faced with destruction, the father decided to sacrifice his daughter to appease the fulmars and the spirits of the deep, but when he threw the poor girl into the foaming water, she held onto the side of the craft with both hands. Unable to break her grasp, the father—now seized with mortal fear for his own life—cut off the tips of Sedna's fingers at the first joints. Instantly the girl's finger-tips turned into whales, the fingernails becoming baleen, the long hornlike substance growing from the jaws of whales and commonly called whalebone.

Though painfully injured, the poor girl clung to her fa-ther's craft, and when his knife fell again, seals filled the water as the second joints of each finger dropped beneath the waves. Finally when her fingerstumps were chopped off, they turned into ground seals (some versions say fish and wal-rus). Believing Sedna had drowned, the fulmars lifted the storm and flew away while Sedna managed to climb back into the boat. During the remainder of the homeward jour-ney, Sedna nourished an understandable urge to even the score with her father, and upon landing, she watched until her father lay down to sleep. Then, calling her dogs, she urged them to chew off her father's feet and hands.

Savage justice having triumphed, the myth ends with a cataclysmic opening of the earth and the disappearance of Sedna, her father, and the house into Adlivun, a place some-where beneath the sea over which Sedna has reigned ever since as the undisputed mistress.

Whether called Old Woman of the Sea or Sedna, the god-dess has been the paramount deity of the Eskimos for un-known ages. Feared and placated through offerings and ritu-als performed by shamans, Sedna is believed responsible for the actions of all the sea spirits and creatures and ranks even higher in the Eskimo pantheon than the Sun and Moon, which were a sister and brother, respectively. Moon brother was passionately and erroneously in love with his Sun sister, upon whom he forced his attentions, after which they fled to the sky, where they have been ever since. Curiously, Eskimo mythology inquires no further into creation or the order of the universe, which is filled with diverse spirits.

Southward of Eskimoland the concept of a supreme being acquires a bit more substance. Raven, it will be remembered from Chapter Two, enjoyed the supernatural ability to be reborn miraculously in the Tsimsyan myth in which he brought sunlight. In a myth of the Haida of the Queen Charlotte Islands, the incarnation of Sky Chief takes on a biblical ring and comes even closer to an aboriginal concept of a supreme being.

The Great Sky Chief of the Haida and Weather Woman

These things almost always happen to people of exalted status, and so it was when the daughter of a chief was on the beach one day, she found a beautiful shell. As the princess held it, she was aware of a sound like that of a baby coming from inside the shell. Sure enough, looking closely the maiden discovered a baby boy.

"See what I have found," the girl said as she entered her father's house. "I found this boy baby inside of a shell on the beach. I will raise him as my son."

Growing miraculously fast, the little boy was soon imitating the warriors who often called upon the chief. One day his foster mother reshaped a copper ornament to resemble a bow. The princess also fashioned several small arrows for the boy, who became a successful hunter. When the princess married, her husband—who understood the circumstances of the wonder child—took the boy to the seashore. As long as the child faced the ocean and sat quietly, the weather was calm and pleasant. On a fishing trip one time with his foster father, the boy suggested a secret and sacred incantation, which caused the fishing line to be shaken so violently that their canoe sped around the home island three times. When the father hauled in his line, an enormous catch of halibut appeared.

Most beautiful of all the clothing his mother prepared for her son was a cloak of bright feathers. As he walked on the beach with his mother one day, the miracle child, who was very handsome and nearly grown, flew high in the air. To his mother's amazement, the boy landed, exchanged his feathered cloak for a bluejay skin, and announced, "I must leave now, Mother. You will see, when the sky is colored gold like my face when my father paints it, the fishing will be good. Good-bye, my mother."

The knowledge that she had raised a supernatural child comforted the lonely princess, and she rejoiced that she still had her husband, who provided for her very well indeed. However, when her husband said, "I, too, must go away," the princess' grief was compounded. "Whenever you sit on the shore and gaze over the ocean and untie your fine robe, the winds will be violent and the waves will be high," her husband told her. "When you pull your robe about you, the winds and waves will be quieted and fine weather will enable your people to be successful in fishing." With these words, the supernatural husband, who was Sky Chief in disguise, flew away as swiftly as had the supernatural boy who had been nurtured in the seashell.

Donated by the Alaska Commercial Company after being collected by R. Neumann at St. Michael on Norton Sound, this old Eskimo mask is about 15 inches high and portrays a man. The large face in the center inside a red circle, the inua, has red lower and black upper lip. Red boots and black stripes decorate the legs. The halo around the body possibly could indicate this is a spirit mask representing Moon Brother, because the encircling hoop usually symbolizes the heavens or upper world. The meaning of the head at top is not known. RLMA by Joseph H. Wherry

Ever since, the princess has been endowed with supernatural power. Called the Weather Woman, she is always close by the sea, where she offers fine feathers—snowflakes—to the deity she found and raised. The snowflakes are messages telling the shell boy that her people are anxious to see his bright gold face which is the Sun.

Southeast on the mainland the Bella Coola are known to have prayed to the Sun, but their Old Woman, Qamits, reigned in the sky as a high deity. Qamits is believed to have been a mythic contemporary of the Haida's Weather Woman.

Greatest of all sea spirits on the Northwest Coast is the mighty Gunah-kah-daht (sometimes called Konakadet) of the Tlingit of southeast Alaska.

The Gunah-kah-daht and the Arrogant Mother-in-Law

Every one should know of this powerful supernatural being of the sea whose spirit helps fishermen and those who hunt seals, sea otters, and whales. Many versions of the myth —some with an ironic twist of humor—are popular on the far Northwest Coast where the being became a beneficent deity.

Long ago a chief named Nah-tse-tla-neh was far from shore hunting sea otter when a sudden storm caused him to fear he would never reach home. Each moment might be his last. Suddenly out of the thrashing waves appeared an enormous manlike figure. The supernatural giant stood almost clear of the waves a minute or so, then sank beneath the surface as slowly as he had appeared.

Recognizing the being as the Gunah-kah-daht, Nah-tse-tla-neh remembered that whoever looked upon him would be assisted, find safety, and eventual greatness. After more terror-filled hours, the canoe was wrecked upon a distant shore. Nah-tse-tla-neh and his companions were uninjured, but all of their supplies were destroyed and they were destitute. Searching the wooded island, they found no other people, no food, and no fresh water. Had the vision of the being been a dream? Were they lost after all?

In a dream he was told to carve eight totems of the Keet (Grampas or killer whale) and that he and his men would be saved. The miracle of all this was that the Keet was so terrible that Nah-tse-tla-neh had never heard of it until that dream. Told that all living sea creatures would flee to the shore when he finished his eight totems and placed them in the sea, Nah-tse-tla-neh worked many days with his stone axe without food to strengthen him. Seals and fish teased him by leaping over the waves; he and his men were starving.

Finally the totems of Keet were completed and thrown into the sea exactly as he had been instructed. When the tide went out, the shore was covered with seals and fish frantically trying to escape the killer whale tribe—the totems had come to life. Now there was plenty of food. Rescued from starvation, the hunters were able to make a new canoe and to return home safely. Ever since that day, when the tall dorsal fin of the Keet is seen, the people know they will have good fishing and sealing. Though essentially evil, the Keet helps those who see the powerful Gunah-kah-daht.

In another version of the same basic tradition, the hero is a much-abused son-in-law who, though given to gambling and

Unfortunately no data was obtained when this Eskimo mask was collected in 1950 somewhere between the Yukon and Kuskokwim rivers on the Bering Sea coast. About 20 inches wide overall, this was probably a shaman's ritual mask. The large face suggests Sedna, high deity and mistress of the sea (represented by the sea otters); the two small faces could be Sun Sister and Moon Brother, although this is conjecture. The four small devices pegged around the bottom most likely are stylized representations of humans. University of Alaska Museum

quite lazy, was a great hunter of seals. However, he and his wife's mother fought constantly. Out of desperation and to have some peace and quiet, he built a small house on a lake, which is said to have been near Wrangell, and began to search for a supernatural being known to live there. With his stone tools he cut a great yellow cedar, made a trap, caught and killed the creature, and put on its skin.

188

With the spirit power of the monster transferred to him, he was able to swim like a fish. When a famine struck his home village, he charged his wife to secrecy, put on his magic skin, caught some large fish, and left them by his mother-in-law's house. The next morning the mother-in-law told all the people she had caught the fish because she was a shaman. The man and his wife laughed secretly, and every morning there were salmon and seals by his mother-in-law's door in great quantity so that everyone in the village had all they could eat. With famine averted, the arrogant mother-in-law enjoyed her growing reputation as a shaman.

One morning when the young man did not return from fishing, his wife heard all the ravens calling. She knew this was a sign that her husband was dead, for the spirits had told him he must return before the raven people awakened. On the beach the grieving wife found a "monster" lying between two whales. Inside the monster's skin the people found the young man. The secret was now out; the widow told who had brought fish to their village to alleviate the famine and how the dead man was a hero with spirit power. He had been overloaded with the two whales and was unable to get home before the ravens called. After a great funeral they placed his bones in a grave box in a tree. Thereafter he was spoken of as the Gunah-kah-daht.

One night while mourning at her husband's grave, the young widow heard him call to her: "Climb upon my back." Then together they went to the supernatural home of the Gunah-kah-daht. Anyone's fortune is assured when this being appears to him on the sea. The Gunah-kah-daht is known all of the way south to Vancouver Island. The deceitful mother-in-law? She died of shame when her fraudulent behavior was exposed.

Kuksu, the Leading California Spirit Being

Nowhere in the West—in all of North America as a matter of fact—was there such a diversity of tribes and linguistic stocks as in California, an Indian cultural region which deserves a separate and popular ethnological volume. Such a variety of tribes and environments in a single region was certain to produce a similar diversity of religious doctrines and mythologies, of which several examples have already been discussed. Escaping our notice thus far has been the Kuksu religion—or cult, as it has been called. Essentially a secret ceremonial organization, Kuksu is also known as Guksu and, in some places, as Big Head. The latter term is believed to have been applied by whites because of a large headdress used in some of the spirit dances. Embracing approximately thirty percent of the area of California, Kuksu included large numbers of the Pomo, Huchnom, Yuki, Coast Miwok, Esselen, Costonoan, and Salinan tribes on the coast, plus the inland Wintun, Miwok, Maidu, Wappo, and the northern bands of the Yokuts. The form of religious devotion centers around the impersonation in dances of Kuksu and lesser spirits.

Headdresses worn by Kuksu-spirit impersonators are enormous, round affairs—sometimes four feet in diameter—with feather-decorated sticks radiating outward from the head. This is complimented with the feather headbands. One of the largest headdresses used in North America, this caused the religion to be termed Big Head in some localities. Directions for the performances of the rituals and the times of celebration are given by the Supreme Being in dreams to "dreamers" some of whom are also shamans. Women as well as men may become dreamers. The author knows such a dreamer, and she is absolutely sincere and devoted to her calling, although she is misunderstood by some of her own people and almost all whites. Shamans and dreamers are treated in the final chapter.

Masks were once used in some of the ceremonial dances performed by the Maidu, according to A. L. Kroeber. In the ancient Kuksu religion, all participants in the dances impersonated spirits, and the masks worn by some dancers ranged from simple grass or tule fabrications to complete deer heads. (Whether other California tribes employed masks is not known, with the exception of the Karok already mentioned.) Keeping secret the personal identities of spirit impersonators was effectively achieved without full face masks, however, by extensive face painting and the popular flicker and yellow hammer headbands used throughout most of California. Worn in the Feather Dance shown herewith, the headbands are customarily drawn so far down upon the forehead and over the eyes that some obscurity of identity is provided.

The high deity of the Kuksu religion closely approximates a supreme being. To the Maidu this deity is Kodoyanpe, which means Earth Namer or Earth Initiator. In relating the Kuksu myth herewith we shall call him Earth Namer for simplicity. The Yuki call the same high deity Taikomol. To the Kato he is Nagaicho. The Wintun call him Olelbis while the Pomo name is Madumda. Earth Namer is regarded as the older or senior brother of Sun, a female, and Moon, a male in Kuksu mythology, but there seems to be no connection with the Eskimo, who apply the same sexes to the heavenly lights. The doctrine names Coyote as another younger brother of Earth Namer. When the latter high deity permitted Coyote to try his own creative abilities, Coyote did all manner of mischief along with some good, as has already been seen. To an orthodox or conservative Kuksu believer, the widespread crediting of Coyote with a status approaching that of an independent deity must smack of heresy. As the

191

Time and place of collection of this Eskimo mask are unknown, nor have details of the symbolization been recorded. It likely represents Sun Sister, for hoops usually indicate upper world. The feathers, fish, and seals (left side) probably signify the minor tornait of the sea, while the small, round eyes suggest a King Island origin. WCHM by Joseph H. Wherry

Kuksu myth unfolds, it appears evident that a theology which began with reverence for a deity enjoying supremacy has been watered down with the acceptance of a pantheon which places the first human, Kuksu, upon a divine plane that must have surpassed his own understanding.

* * *

Water was everywhere in the beginning when Father of the Secret Society and Turtle came floating out of the North on a raft. No one knows where they came from. Suddenly a rope of feathers dropped out of the sky to the raft, and down climbed Earth Namer. He came to the raft. His body glowed brightly but his face was covered with something. No one said anything for a long time; they just sat.

"Where are you from?" Turtle finally said.

"From above," Earth Namer answered.

"Can you make dry land?" pleaded Turtle. "I would like to get out of the water."

Earth Namer just sat; he did not answer.

"Will there be people?" Turtle asked after awhile. "When will there be people?"

"If you want dry land," Earth Namer finally said, "I must have some earth to make it of. How can we get some?"

Turtle had an idea. "Tie a rope to me and I will dive deep down into the water and get some earth," he told Earth Namer, who got a rope.

"When I jerk the rope twice," said Turtle, "pull me up, because I will have a load of earth." And as he dived, Father of the Secret Society gave a great shout.

After about six years, Turtle yanked the rope two times and Earth Namer pulled him up to the raft. "Where is your load of earth?" Earth Namer asked.

"All I have is under my fingernails," Turtle replied. He was covered all over with slime because of his long journey.

From beneath his left armpit Earth Namer pulled a stone knife with which he removed the earth from under Turtle's nails. Rolling the bit of earth into a ball, he placed it on the raft and then he sat down. Earth Namer waited. When he looked the third time the ball of earth had grown as large as Earth Namer's arms could reach. After another wait, Earth Namer looked the fourth time, and the ball had grown as big as the world is now and there were mountains everywhere. The raft was ashore at Tadoiko, which is about ten miles southeast of Chico, California.

"I need light so I can see," Turtle complained. "Can you make some light?"

"We should get off the raft," said Earth Namer, and all three stepped onto the land. Father of the Secret Society was very quiet; he said nothing—just stepped on land.

"Look to the East," said Earth Namer. As he pointed, light began rising. "My sister, the Sun, rises." As daylight came, Father of the Secret Society got very excited. Ordered by Earth Namer to travel a certain way, Sun rose, passed overhead, and then went down. As darkness fell, Father of the Secret Society began to jump around and yell.

"Now it is time for my Moon brother to come up," said Earth Namer, and when Moon rose, his companions said, "That is good."

Earth Namer then called each star by its name and told it where to go in the sky. After a while Turtle wondered what should be done next, and Earth Namer made a tree with many kinds of acorns. The tree was named Hukimtsa. Father of the Secret Society and Turtle enjoyed the tree's shade for two whole days. The next day they explored the new world and saw a ball of fire traveling everywhere; that was Earth Namer. During the day Coyote emerged from the ground, and so did his dog, Rattlesnake. Coyote, because he was really Earth Namer's younger brother, could see Earth Namer's face when they all assembled together at Tadoiko at sundown. Everyone now built a house, but Earth Namer's was secret; the others were not allowed inside. These were the first houses at Tadoiko, which was the middle of the world. Next Earth Namer made more trees and plants and all of the animals and birds. He made them from mud and molded each one while Turtle watched and offered advice.

Several days later Earth Namer and Coyote were at the hills called Marysville Buttes, where they built another house.

"Now it is time for people," Earth Namer announced. "Now I am going to make them!" About five hours before sunset Earth Namer took some red-colored dirt with which he mixed some water. While Coyote watched, Earth Namer molded a man and a woman. He placed the man on his right side, the woman on his left on the house floor. "Now I will lie down on my back and sweat," said Earth Namer.

All night Earth Namer lay quietly; he just sweated. When the woman moved and tickled him the next morning, Earth Namer pretended not to notice and kept very still. At the proper time he stood up and stuck a stick of greasewood into the earth floor. Immediately the stick flamed brightly. By the firelight Earth Namer and Coyote saw that Kuksu and Morning Star Woman were pure white with black hair and pink eyes. The first man and woman were very beautiful except for their hands.

"How shall I make their hands?" said Earth Namer.

"Make their hands like my paws" Coyote suggested.

"No, they must have fingers like mine so they can climb trees and make things," Earth Namer decided, and so their hands were formed. (It will be remembered from Chapter Two that another myth has Coyote making people with hands like Lizard's. Many myths incorporate the creativity of the Kuksu religion's Earth Namer—or Earth Initiator, depending upon the tribal version—into the Coyote complex.)

Having observed his older brother, Coyote said, "Now *I* will make some people." But even then, so long ago, Coyote was erratic and unpredictable. Though he sweated and lay flat on his back quietly at Marysville Buttes, he laughed when the woman tickled his side. Because of this mistake, the people Coyote made had dark eyes and their skins were darker, too.

195

"Your people are not like Kuksu and Morning Star Woman," Earth Namer told him. "You should not have laughed!"

"I did not laugh," Coyote lied. "I did not laugh." And with this lie Coyote brought deceit into the world.* Coyote's people were the first Indians.

Soon there were many people, and food of all kinds was plentiful. Everyone was healthy and illness and death were unknown. Earth Namer now came very seldom. When he did, his visits were secret and at night and only to Kuksu to teach him the songs, dances, and ceremonies. Some say Father of the Secret Society talked with Earth Namer also.

"Call all of the people together tomorrow morning," Earth Namer said one night, "and lead them to the lake. On the way to the lake you, Kuksu, will become very old."

Sure enough, when Kuksu arrived at the lake the next morning, he was very old and feeble and he fell into the lake. When Kuksu sank beneath the water's surface, there was a violent earthquake which shook the earth and made great waves. As the ground shook, there was a mighty roaring sound underneath and thunder in the sky.

Then, without warning, Kuksu appeared from the lake and he was young again. As Kuksu came out of the water, Earth Namer also appeared before all the people and told them to follow his teachings and to go to the lake when old age came upon them. Earth Namer promised if they would go into the water, they would be made young just as Kuksu had been. That night Earth Namer went away secretly; he just went up.

Now Coyote decided he should visit the women. "It is not

* Could this be an ancient aboriginal illustration of original sin? All available evidence points to total lack of influence by early Christian missionaries in the Kuksu religion. Hence, this and other similarities with Judaic-Christian doctrines are all the more interesting.

196

Shamans used masks like this when spirit-talking to the moon. Collected many years ago by Charles L. Hall from the "Lower Yukon or Northwest Bering Sea," an indefinite source. From top to bottom the mask measures 25 inches. Described as the "girl in the moon," this mask suggests a lower Yukon River and Norton Sound myth version saying that the pursued maiden became Moon Sister while her pursuing brother became Sun—the opposite of the more traditional myth related in the accompanying text. The flat nose and facial shape is also favored by the westernmost Athabaskan Indians in Alaska. Eye outlines, brows, and chin-tatoo marks are black. Board around face shows blue and red paint. Curved lip labret and ears are separate carvings. RLMA by Joseph H. Wherry

right that you should place your baskets outside your houses at night and find them filled with food at dawn," he told them. "Besides," he raved on, "it would just be better if everybody worked, grew old, died, and made room for his children. We must have a burning."

"But what is a burning?" someone asked. Coyote explained that all the people should gather and begin with a

197

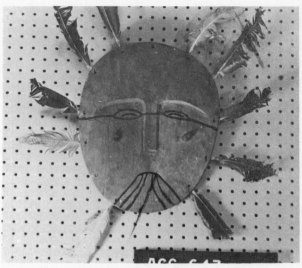

Another flat-nosed mask, but less refined than the other example. Collected in the 1920s, this type of mask is "made by the lower Yukon Eskimo and also the Ingalik Indians in the Anvik-Holy Cross area." The face is 15 inches long and painted red. The being portrayed is not known. University of Alaska Museum

foot race. Hearing this, Rattlesnake went to Kuksu, who agreed that Coyote would spoil everything. Kuksu was unhappy.

"I have a plan," said Rattlesnake, who went to a rock near the path and hid. Fastest runner of all was Coyote's son, and as he passed Rattlesnake, he was bitten on the foot. In a few minutes Coyote's son was dead. Picking up his son, Coyote put him in the lake, but nothing happened. Offerings of beads on the fifth day did not help when Kuksu came outside to the lake.

"Death has come to us and we must bury Coyote's son," Kuksu told the people. "You must do this until the world is remade."

A year later the people had a burning. All those who had lost loved ones through death made offerings of valuables and there was a great cry and a mourning ceremony. "This is the way all people must do," Kuksu told them.

One night during the long ceremony Earth Namer came to Kuksu. "Tomorrow there will be many languages," Earth Namer said, "and you must name the tribes and tell them where to live, how to make their living houses and dance houses, how to hunt and gather acorns."

Kuksu did as instructed by Earth Namer. All the people departed and Kuksu and his wife, Morning Star Woman, were the only ones living at Tadoiko. After a time Kuksu's wife went away and Kuksu went to the sacred house, entered the door on the West, and sat down on the south side near the center pole.

"Hello," someone sitting on the north side said. It was the spirit of Coyote's son. Now Kuksu knew that he himself was also dead. When Coyote came to the door, he was not allowed to enter. Just seeing Kuksu and his son eating spirit food made the rascal hungry.

"Every bad thing that has happened is your fault, Coyote," Kuksu told him. "Until Earth Namer returns, people must work, grow old, die, and go to the spirit world, the land of the dead."

"But I'm hungry. Please give me some of your food," Coyote begged.

"No," retorted Kuksu, "this is spirit food. Go tell all of the people what I have told you," Kuksu ordered, and Coyote did as he was told.

Kuksu and the son of Coyote ate spirit food until night. Then they just went up to the spirit land of the dead as Earth Namer had said they would, and Father of the Secret Society was left to guide the people in the correct ceremonies.

* * *

Through the ages—precisely how long no one really knows—Kuksu took on a messianic flavor not unlike that of Quetzalcoatl of Mexico. Modified to suit the needs of the California Indians during the 1870–91 Ghost Dance revivialistic cult which swept across half of the nation, modern variants such as the Bole Maru and the Hesi sub-cults brought new prestige to the old Kuksu religion, which still has many adherents.

Turquoise Woman—High Navajo Deity

After the ways of life and death were determined, many monsters appeared. Some say that First Man and First Woman created them to punish the people for their selfishness and foolishness. In any event the monsters killed so many people that finally only a few people and Salt Woman remained alive.

One day the people saw Earth and Sky meet. When First Woman and Salt Woman went to a mountaintop, they found a tiny turquoise figure shaped like a woman. They wondered what it meant. Not long afterward a distant voice called. The voice grew louder. Suddenly one of the Holy Ones came to them.

"Bring the turquoise to Tso-lihi, the mountaintop in the middle of the world, twelve days from now," Talking God said.

On Tso-lihi the people marveled at the sight of the Holy Ones standing in a circle with an opening on the East. Awaiting them were Hastyehogan, the Hogan God; Ganaskidi, the Harvest God who is also called Mountain Sheep God; Niltsi, the God of Wind; and all of the other "yei" except Hastye-

yalti, the Father of the Gods, who is called Talking God.
Then toward the East, where the Daylight People dwelled,
they saw Talking God. He came quickly into the circle, and
in his hands was another tiny figure made of a white shell.
Now the Holy Ones took the tiny turquoise figure from the
people and placed it alongside the white shell figure on a ceremonial deerskin in the center of the circle. Two more things
were laid upon the sacred skin: an ear of white corn and another ear of yellow. Over the four perfect things the Holy
Ones placed another deerskin for a cover, and then, while
they sang holy songs, the Wind God Niltsi danced and blew
the breath of life between the buckskins.

After singing four times, the Holy Ones lifted the top deerskin. On the bottom skin breathed four living beings. Turquoise Woman, who was called Estanatlehi, her sister,
White Shell Woman, who was called Yolkaiestsan, White
Corn Boy, and Yellow Corn Girl. The Holy Ones departed
after the ceremony, telling Turquoise Woman and White
Shell Woman to remain on the mountain, but taking White
Corn Boy and Yellow Corn Girl with them to their holy
place.

(In variants of this myth, Turquoise Woman and White
Shell Woman are but different aspects of the same supernatural being. In one myth, Estanatlehi is discovered as a baby
on the mountain by First Woman, who takes her home where
she grows to maturity in four days, after which she meets
Sun disguised as a human. Becoming Sun's wife, Estanatlehi
gives birth—again in four days—to the same twin Warrior
Gods who become the saviours of the people.)

On the mountaintop one warm day, Turquoise Woman
faced the East. Then, lying down, she reveled in the warm
rays of sunshine. Meanwhile White Shell Woman went beneath the waterfall and enjoyed the cool stream as it flowed
over her. Four days later Talking God and Hogan God came

201

to the sacred sisters to assist them as they gave birth to the boys Nayenezgani and Tobadsistsini. In another four days the boys were grown and the "yei" taught them how to run fast around the mountain. Then the mothers made bows and arrows for Nayenezgani, which means Elder Brother, and Tobadsistsini, which means Younger Brother. Though the mothers taught their sons how to hunt, they also warned them not to go far away. Disregarding the warning, the two young gods dared to venture far afield, and one day they returned with fear in their hearts and questions on their tongues.

"We saw birds with black feathers and long, white tails flying over us," they said. "There were other birds, small and black all over, and animals which peered at us from behind bushes and red-headed birds in trees. Who are they?"

"Those birds are magpies, crows, and buzzards," the mothers explained, "and the sneaking animals are coyotes. All of them are evil spies of the dreadful monster Yeitso and of Teelget, the flesheating antelope [synonymous with the monster elk in the Jicarilla-Apache myth in Chapter Five], and of the other terrible creatures who are devouring the people." Turquoise Woman and White Shell Woman explained how the enemy gods must be avoided until the boys had learned how to destroy them.

"We must see our father," the young Warrior Gods said to each other. "He will tell us how to destroy the monsters." (From this point in the myth White Shell Woman seems to merge into oneness with Turquoise Woman.)

Again they went hunting, and when they saw smoke rising from a hole in the earth, they entered and discovered they were in the presence of Nastseestsan, the Spider Woman.

"We search for our father," the Warrior Gods explained.

"You must eat," Spider Woman said, and as they ate, she told them that their father, Tsohanoai the Sun (some say

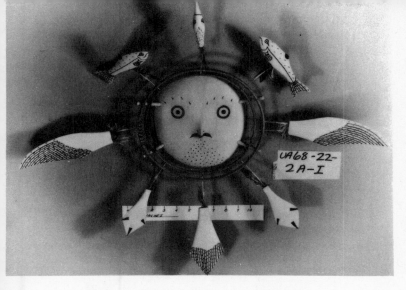

Made on Nunivak Island in 1967, this Eskimo mask is based upon traditional concepts but is made primarily for the tourist trade. Hence the almost plastic-like, too-smooth finish. This mask is the only tourist-oriented artifact illustrated in this volume. Symbolized almost too realistically is Arctic Owl's spirit, who imparts healing power to shamans and hunting and fishing skills to ordinary folk. The mask is white painted with black details. University of Alaska Museum

Sun Bearer, which is probably more accurate) lived far to the West beyond the Sacred Mountains.

"The journey is full of dangers," Spider Woman said. "Take these feathers which are from the bodies of the monsters, follow my instructions closely, and you will find your father's house." Then she taught them prayers and holy songs to use whenever danger threatened them.

"Walk the pollen path of peace; be alert, quiet, and careful," Spider Woman cautioned. "That is the way of happiness." And she gave them pollen and told them how to use it.

On the long journey they had to run between rocks that tried to roll over them, go through a swampy forest of reeds with knifelike edges which tried to slash their bodies, and

203

Because Eskimo women generally were forbidden to wear face masks, many wore miniatures on their fingers during dances. The tiny carvings—these are about 4 inches high—duplicated the supernaturals on masks; these may depict Sun Sister, although this interpretation is not definite. Sometimes called "finger masks," this pair were looped over two fingers; the left one is broken. RLMA by Joseph H. Wherry

cross a field of cactus with sharp protruding spines everywhere. Finally they came to a vast desert where the swirling sands were fiery hot. Their only defense against the ordeal was the songs and prayers Spider Woman had taught them, and when they repeated the songs and prayers, they heard a voice saying, "Go to your father's house."

Next they came to a great water. The Holy Ones had anticipated the quest of the Warrior Gods. On a rainbow they bridged the water to a turquoise house, the door of which was guarded by two enormous bears. With a sprinkling of their pollen, the brothers put the bears to sleep. With prayer and pollen a pair of big snakes, lightning bolts, and guardian winds were also quieted as the brothers entered the house.

"We are searching for our father, Sun Bearer," the brothers said to the hostile woman seated on the side of the house facing to the East.

"My husband, Sun Bearer, kills all who enter," the woman said. "However, I will conceal you." And she hid them inside of dark clouds above the entrance.

At sundown Sun Bearer entered, and the two Warrior Gods watched him as he placed the great Sun disc on the west wall, where it gradually lost its brilliance as night fell.

Sun Bearer asked his wife about the footprints he'd seen as he approached his home.

"Two young gods who say they are your sons," the woman told Sun Bearer, and she caused the clouds to fall away.

In a rage, Sun Bearer slammed the brothers against the walls in each of the four directions. They were unhurt despite the long sharp turquoise points on the walls. Then Sun Bearer placed the brothers in his sweathouse, where they were subjected to a searing heat. Four times Sun Bearer did this to test the young gods.

"You are truly the sons of Sun," Sun Bearer said when he saw how the young gods survived the trials without hurt. Then Sun Bearer had them washed, and the young gods' bodies glowed like the Sun, their father. After ceremonies welcoming them, Sun Bearer said, "Tell me why you have come, my sons. What can I do for the sons of Turquoise Woman?"

The twin Warrior Gods realized they had been tested in each of the four directions and that the purifying inferno of the sweathouse had further confirmed their supernatural kinship with Sun Bearer. Finally they spoke: "The people are being destroyed by monsters. We have come for weapons and instructions. Please help us."

Sun Bearer pondered before responding because the monsters—the Enemy Gods—were the children he had fathered during the Creation before the people had emerged, and some were his grandchildren. Finally he spoke: "Yes, the monsters must be destroyed so the people can live. The first one you must conquer is Yeitso, the monster in the East who drinks dry the lake by the mountain Tso-lihi. Kill Yeitso and drought will threaten the people no longer." (A parallel to Yeitso in Pueblo mythology is the Cloud Eater story related in Chapter Four in which the Old Woman and Ahaiyuta are Zuni counterparts of Turquoise Woman and either of the Warrior Gods.)

Then the Sun Bearer gave his sons suits of flint armor, stone clubs and knives, lightning arrows, and rainbows to help them. Some say Sun Bearer also gave them thunderbolts and containers of wind. After bidding his sons farewell, he took them to the opening in the sky and, placing them on lightning, sent them down to the top of Tso-lihi, the jewel-covered mountain in the middle of the world. There the Holy Ones met them and, during the night, told them how to conquer Yeitso, who was so large that one of his steps was as far as one of the people could walk in a day. At sunrise the young gods heard the sound of thunder and saw the monster's head rise above the flat, dark sacred mountain Tsisnad-zini in the East where Rock Crystal Boy and Rock Crystal Girl had come to life after the emergence. At high noon the head of Yeitso appeared above sacred Tsot-sil, the Great Mountain at the South which is the abode of Turquoise Boy and Turquoise Girl. Late in the afternoon the monster's head reared over the sacred yellow mountain in the West, Doko-slid, which today is called Cloud Water Mountain and on which live White Corn Boy and Yellow Corn Girl, whom the Holy Ones created at the same time as the mothers of the twin Warrior Gods. Abalone shells were on this peak. Then, after a long day of waiting, the young gods saw Yeitso coming over the sacred mountain of the North, Depent-tsa, which

206

The Bella Coola regarded the sun as a
manifestation of the supreme deity. Over
25 inches in diameter and showing a
woman in the sun, the myth illustrated may
be related to that of Weather Woman,
the Haida supernatural. The mask has
shredded-cedar-bark hair with red, white,
black, and blue paint. It was collected before 1897 by Franz Boas and George Hunt.
AMNH by Joseph H. Wherry

was thusly named by the Holy Ones because of a covering of fine black coal. On it live Pollen Boy and Grasshopper Girl, who guard herds of bighorn sheep. Slowly down the North mountain came Yeitso, straight to the lake near the middle of the world, where he bent down with one arm resting on the sacred mountain of the South, the other on the North from whence he had come.

"What boys are these?" the monster roared when he saw their reflections in the last drops of water as he drank the lake dry.

"What monster do we see?" Elder Brother, Nayenezgani, called back to the monster.

Yeitso's reply was to throw his thunderbolts at the young gods, who dodged easily by using their rainbows. Both brothers now shot their lightning arrows at the head of their enemy. Falling toward the East and South, the monster roared. His armor fell away but he stood up again. Another volley of arrows to his body felled him to the West and North, where he lay motionless. Now the young gods drew the great stone knives and cut off Yeitso's head, keeping his scalp as a trophy to show their mothers. When the blood gushed forth with great force, it made a stream across the valley.

"Do not let Yeitso's blood reach any of the other monsters," came the voice of Niltsi, the Wind God. "Cut through the stream with your knife. Quickly!"

And quickly the brothers made a deep slash in the ground across the stream of blood, as the Wind God explained that other monsters would replace Yeitso's head and revive him if any of his blood came to them. Red and black rocks in Navajoland today, are the remains of Yeitso's blood from that first day of battle against the monster Enemy Gods..

Hastening to their mothers, Turquoise Woman and White Shell Woman, the young gods asked about more monsters to attle. Talking God came to them and told Younger Brother to protect the mothers while Elder Brother found and slew Teelget, the flesh-eating antelope. Upon returning victoriously to his mother's hogan, Elder Brother was received with great joy and called Killer of Enemy Monsters. Early the following morning he set out to destroy the Tsenahali, the giant eagles. After the battle, all of the eagles' feathers became birds. (Again we have similar Apache traditions, as related in Chapter Five.)

The next enemy monster challenged by Elder Brother was Kicking Giant, whose hair secured him to the rocks to prevent his falling. People who traveled in the mountains were always kicked off the path to their deaths by this enemy. When the giant tried four times to kick the young Killer of Enemy Monsters off the mountain, the young god cut the giant's hair off, causing him to fall. Far below, his wife and children mistook him for one of his victims and roasted him. They were cannibals. Some say that Kicking Giant's family were changed into birds that eat waste matter.

Perhaps the most fiendish of all the enemies of the people were the Bin-aye Ahani, whose protruding eyes flashed killing bolts of lightning at all who met them in the mountains of the North. Upon entering their house, Elder Brother summoned all of his spirit power and their lightning stares bounced off his flint armor. He threw salt into the fire pit, and when the evil monsters were blinded he cut off their heads with his stone knife. Scalping all of these enemies, the victor hurried home for a scalp dance.

Yeitso was the one with many surviving children who were beginning to threaten the people. Both young Warrior Gods destroyed them with the winds from the container Sun Bearer, their father, had given to them. The Great Bear who tracked everyone who passed near any of the four entrances to his den was confused by Elder Brother's speed and he lost

Dramatic presentations of mythical events required impressive masks like this 30-inch-diameter Kwakiutl example, which depicts Killer Whale against Sun painted black, blue, green, red, and white. Collected by Samuel A. Barrett in 1915. MPM by Joseph H. Wherry

his head to the stone knife. Parts of the head became various plants and herbs when thrown to the four directions. One of the last monsters was Traveling Stone, which could smell anyone approaching; it could turn itself into water or hurl small particles with fatal results. Elder Brother compromised with this threat and exacted a pledge from Traveling Stone to become a supplier of water. Some say that it became the beneficent Water Sprinkler God. Traveling Stone has kept its word. After the foregoing encounters the young Warrior Gods were exhausted and rested four days. Then they went to their father's other abode in the East, another turquoise house beside another sea. When they requested a renewal of their strength, Sun Bearer asked them to invite *their* mother, Estanatlehi the Turquoise Woman, to come to a new turquoise palace on an island in the ocean of the West. The sons consented, and bearing gifts for their mother—"hard goods" like jewels and hailstones and "soft goods" like eagle down and the finest cloths—they departed with restored strength.

Delighted with the gifts, Turquoise Woman made a storm over the world which destroyed the remaining monsters, created all of the trees, animals, and things the people would need, and changed the face of the earth. Knowing more people were needed, she filled a basket with white corn flour and another with yellow corn flour. From her breasts she shook dust into each basket and, adding water, she stirred the supernatural mixtures and moulded a man from the white flour and a woman from the yellow flour. Nurtured through the night between sacred buckskins, they were alive at sunrise. In four days the new couple had children who were grown in another four days. Every four days there were more new people—the first four Navajo clans, each of which lived in a house at one of the four directions.

"Now I will go to live in the turquoise house on the western island in the great water," Turquoise Woman told her sons. On the journey to the West she created four more couples to complete the clans of the Navajo nation and sent them back to the world between the Four Sacred Mountains with puma and bear as their hunters and protectors. Some say that a great snake and a turtle were also provided as aids for the new people. When Turquoise Woman was satisfied with her new creation, when the new people had learned how to make hogans, how to weave, cook, gather and hunt food,

Realistic masks were used at potlatches by the Haida to represent clan ancestors and human participants in mythical events. Portraying an affluent woman wearing a labret in her lower lip, the top mask (NMC) could represent the supernatural Weather Woman. The man's mask (CNHM) shows face painting symbolizing Eagle's spirit.
Joseph H. Wherry

how to plant corn of the colors of the Six Directions (this includes Zenith and Nadir), Turquoise Woman began to live in splendor in the fabulous turquoise house prepared for her by Sun Bearer. As for her (foster) parents, First Man and First Woman, they went to another turquoise house somewhere near sacred Tsisnad-zini in the East.

For many ages the Navajo have also called their Turquoise Woman by another name—Changing Woman. Ever living, ever lovely, ever young just as the year renews itself, Estanatlehi the Changing Woman, great mother of the great Navajo nation gave—and gives—her people everything that is good. With the Holy People and the two young Warrior Gods she is painted in the sand with pollen, finely ground stones, herbs, and other essences of life when the great mysteries are invoked in the chants for the healing of bodies and the renewal of souls. Though her abode is on an island in the western waters, Turquoise Woman is constantly present to the Navajo who chooses to live in the traditional way. The original eight clans created by Turquoise Woman eventually expanded to around fifty, some with Pueblo origins.

To the linguistically related Apache nation, Turquoise Woman (Estanatlehi) becomes Ihsta-nedleheh, Changing Woman (another similarity to the Navajo designation). Her sons, Child of the Water and Killer of Monsters, had adventures very much like those of their Navajo counterparts. Indeed the Apache creation myth is scarcely distinguishable from that of their more populous related nation. Changing Woman is personified in the girls' puberty rite as White Painted Woman, and her attributes are social as well as religious. In the latter aspect, this goddess is the highest deity of the Apache, who also regard her as the young and lovely beneficent provider of all needs forever.

The Deities of the Pueblos

Even more complex is the mythology of the village tribes, the Pueblo descendants of the ancient city builders and cultivators who preceded the Athabaskan-speaking Navajo and Apache tribes into the Southwest Region. Indeed, anthropologists tend to agree that the Navajo/Apache traditions and sacred pantheons have been influenced greatly by those of the Pueblo tribes. Many of the Pueblo deities closely approach the stature of a supreme being.

For example Sho'tokunungwa, the Hopi (also called Moqui) Star God is the God of War and Lightning, but he is a step below Massau'u, the Skeleton Man, who is God of Life and Death and is the high deity. Pautiwa, the Sun, assisted in the destruction of the monsters, the Soyoko, who threatened the human race after emergence upon the earth. To the Zuni, their Pautiwa presides over all of the other gods in a manner similar to Talking God of the Navajo, but A'wonawil'ona is an even higher female deity who exercises creative will and protection over the people headed by Poshaiyangkyo, who was First Man and Father of Medicine. In the pantheon of the Keres people, Paiyatemu (Sun Youth) fathered twin war gods and is the leading god, but Thinking Woman (Sus'sistinako) created the world "by thinking outward into space—and she is supreme," as Hamilton Tyler says in his *Pueblo Gods and Myths*, which the author recommends as the most thoroughly delineative book available on the mythology of the Pueblo dwellers. Corn Mother (Iyatiku) is but another aspect of the creative principle; she and her sister Naotsete mothered Masewi and Oyoyewi, the older and younger brothers who are the Twin War Gods who went forth and destroyed the Skoyo (monsters).

The above examples of Pueblo deities will serve to illus-

214

These Pomo lads may become Big Head or Kuksu dancers in a native religion that once embraced a third of California. Note that the flicker-feather headband is worn very low over the eyes. The youths clutch a reed whistle as they dance. Joseph H. Wherry

trate the probable foundation upon which the Navajo mythology is based. However, the outstanding characteristic of the Pueblo cosmos is that each Pueblo tribe, indeed each village in some instances, is still located at or very near where their primal ancestors emerged from the previous worlds. Any traditional migrations were for very short distances, although the Cochiti myth of their origin after emergence from Shipap (as related in Chapter Six) may seem to be at vari-

ance with this almost universal belief among the Pueblo
tribes. Beginnings and endings—or deaths—are all combined within the restricted area occupied by the pueblo concerned. At death the dead return to the underworld land of
the dead at a secret place near the area where they lived out
their lives.

Earth is Mother—Sky personified by Sun is Father. All
other high deities are offspring of these primal parents, and
they, in turn, created The People.

Masks and Their Use in Religious Ceremonies

asks are important in the traditional religious and healing ceremonies of Indians in the West, where more or less established village life facilitated an intensity of formal religious practices. In many respects, the masks took the place, in the aboriginal cultures, of the ikons and other sacred objects of the religious orders of the Old World. What many people of European background fail—or refuse—to appreciate is that the sacred ceremonial objects of the original Americans signified the very real presence of spirits and deities in much the same way as do the crucifixes, chalices, altars, and candles of the faiths encompassed in the Judaic-Christian ethic. In other words, the masks were more than representative symbols of spirits and powers; they were holy objects, and when worn, they had the power to transform the wearer into the spirit or deity portrayed. The wearer usually purified himself by bathing, fasting, and meditating before putting on the mask and again after the ceremony was concluded. Often the masks themselves were ceremonially purified—or sanctified—be-

217

fore being stored away in secret places until the next occasion for their use. But to understand the masks, we must consider the religious practices that grew out of the mythology.

Religious intensity—and the accompanying widespread use of masks—in the American and Canadian West was concentrated in the Arctic, on the Northwest Coast, and in the Southwest regions, which were defined in the opening chapter. Elsewhere religion was less formalized with the exception of California. Of course distinctions must be made between the two principle reasons for religious practice: the exorcism of evil or negative influences and the invocation of positive or beneficent influences.

To American Indians, supernatural powers, the gods, deities, and spirits themselves were not always divided into good and bad. The more common attitude toward the supernatural powers was based upon *how* the powers were used. Power was power—a spiritual force granted by one or more of a host of supernaturals—and the user of power employed it for either beneficial or negative purposes. The power or force in itself was neither good nor bad; the user determined whether the end result of invoking it would be good or evil. The selfish use of power for personal and negative reasons, witchcraft, was considered evil and was punished as a crime by Indians everywhere. Practitioners of evil were believed to employ the same supernatural powers for their nefarious purposes as did those intent upon producing good results. The traditional myths provided the framework of morality and explained the powers, while the masks made the powers visible in the ceremonies when the wearer became *one* with the spiritual power portrayed.

To further understand the philosophy of the Indians of the West, however, we must recognize a traditional tenet of their

218

Eskimo villagers performing a traditional masked dance for visitors to their community house in King Island Village near Nome. The bad shaman on the left with sulky, heavy lower lip fights a word-and-spirit battle with the good shaman on right, who has a thick upper lip. Elbow-length gloves are decorated with puffin beaks which rattle and symbolize hailstones a shaman heard when he saw spirits in the clouds. King Islanders go to Nome for summer work and return for winter. State of Alaska Travel Division

philosophy of life: all of nature is good, and because man is a part of the whole of nature, he is also good unless he falls prey to selfishness. It was alien to their thinking that the latter failing indicated what is regarded as original sin by the Christian faith. Consequently the possibility of original sin never occurred to the Indian. On the other hand, Indians believed that such physical discomforts as poverty were due to the capricious behavior of various spirits or of individuals

219

Red beak and blue dots on some obscure supernatural bird's forehead distinguish this 15-inch-high mask collected about 1880 by the Alaska Commercial Company. The transverse line across the top of the upper part of the beak is a double thong of seal sinew the meaning of which is not known. Note that many of the peg teeth are missing. From Cape Prince of Wales to the Aleutian Islands, shamans' masks similar to this were popular, but the inua or inner spirit inside the mouth of the supernatural creature is a bit out of the ordinary. RLMA by Joseph H. Wherry

who used their spiritual resources for their own evil purposes. Navajo mythology goes further and tells how the twin Warrior Gods were dispatched on one final mission by Turquoise Woman to destroy Disease, Hunger, Old Age, and Poverty. Each of these conditions was incarnate in a male being and his wife, who epitomized the extreme degradation of the condition concerned. As the Warrior Gods approached each couple in turn and made ready to deal the killing blow, the beings cautioned the young gods to consider mankind's alternative. For example, Poverty said that without his presence, the people would grow lazy and would have

220

no incentive to work diligently to better themselves. The culmination of the quest to destroy the aboriginal versions of the Four Horsemen was to allow them to exist, because without them the people would never appreciate life and the bounties of nature. These traditions fostered the belief that such misfortunes as disease and poverty were not the consequences of sin—although misfortune could be caused by violating a taboo—but were caused by external forces over which the afflicted individual had little or no control. This attitude prevailed quite generally throughout the West and led to ceremonies of exorcism or placation designed to remove or disable the afflicting spirit or substance. The other purpose of rituals was to invoke the blessings of powers capable of bringing prosperity, health, and happiness.

Religious Practice

Indian religious practices are based upon the fundamentals of their traditional mythology, salient examples of which have been related. The individual feels himself dependent upon spirit power—some have called this magic—believed to reside in various deities, birds, animals, plants, or in geological features like the sacred Eye-eek-wi rock in the Klamath River near its junction with the Trinity in Yurok country. When travelers passed the rock, a nature spirit called a greeting.

Even more famous as a sacred shrine was the Hee-hee rock near the Canadian border in the land of the Okanogan tribe, which, tradition says, was once the daughter of a Kalispel chief. Coyote turned the maiden into her rock likeness because she rebuked him for meddling in an argument between three Okanogan brothers, each of whom wanted to marry her. Three mountains west of the rock are the warrior brothers; the tallest is Mount Chopaka. As she was turning to rock, the maiden hurled her basketful of tasty camas roots back into her own Kalispel country and said that camas never would grow in the Okanogan valley. For ages before the coming of the whites, Indians took gifts to the rock figure— also called Camas Woman—which is said to have assured good fortune. Early in this century a rancher broke Camas Woman to pieces. Having violated an ancient Indian taboo, the man was killed shortly afterward in an accident when his team of horses bolted. Many such sacred places were the abode of spirits and were as regionally important as the Navajo's Four Sacred Mountains in the Southwest.

Everywhere the medicine man or shaman (a word with roots in Asia) was the center of religious activity. The Eskimo angakok was kept busy warding off the temperamental Sedna and the lesser tornait (spirits) who controlled illness, the supply of game animals, and the like. Eskimo, Aleut, and Northwest Coast tribes placed great store in the efficacy of the guardian spirits that were symbolized on countless masks, many of which are illustrated photographically and explained throughout this volume. In fact the Eskimo and Northwest Coast tribes developed the art of mask making to a higher degree than elsewhere in the United States or Canada, with the exception of the Pueblo tribes. The masks of the latter, as mentioned earlier must be illustrated with drawings to avoid violating tribal taboos which prevent publication of exact photographic reproductions. Guardian spirits were obtained by extended quests—often lasting weeks—during which the supplicant fasted, bathed, meditated, and invoked the powers of nature. Visions and dreams were instrumental in acquiring such tutelary spirits, who appeared in their animal or bird forms, taught the individual

222

*Very old, this photograph was made in lat-
ter half of nineteenth century by an unknown photographer during a performance
by a Kwakiutl shamans' society. The long
beak—at least 6 feet—in the middle of the
photo is probably of the mythical Hohoq
bird, who lives in the mountains, eats people, and was portrayed by cannibal dancers
who sometimes became possessed and ran
amuk biting onlookers. Shredded red cedar
bark hid the faces of the shamans, keeping
their identities secret. The Bella Coola and
Nootka had similar performances. Various
crests are on the carved house totem posts
in the background.* RLMA by Joseph H.
Wherry

Such a complicated mask must have been owned by a successful and wealthy Kwakiutl shaman. Above the face piece, the design of which makes definite creature identification troublesome, is what appears to be the likeness of Sandhill Crane with a string-operated beak which clacked loudly, a jointed neck that can be straightened to an impressive height, and arm-like wings that flap grotesquely. The face piece can symbolize the supernatural bird's inner human spirit. Sandhill Crane was often the guardian spirit of women who could be shamans. DAM by Joseph H. Wherry

songs and personal rituals, and gave directions for successful living and service to the people. The ways in which the spirits came and bestowed their powers were curiously similar to incidents in the lives of the early Christian saints and mystics of the world's great religions.

When the possessor of one or more powerful tutelary spirits appeared to have unusual psychic or healing power, he or she could become a shaman. Among the Tlingit and Haida of southeast Alaska and British Columbia, the spirit power could be acquired through heredity from one's uncles —the descent being reckoned matrilinealy. The Tsimsyan, Kwakiutl, Bella Coola, Nootka, and Coast Salish tribes recognized the spirit quest as the primary means of ordination. Customarily shamans fell into two categories: those who specialized in curing sickness and retrieving lost souls—the vitality or life forces—and those who controlled the elements, the food supply, and the like. Shaman power was often possessed by chiefs or by those closely related to chiefs. Thus success in war, when relocating the village, or when embarking upon clan or tribal enterprises like building a new plank house or carving a totem pole was more readily assured when chief and shaman had a mutually cooperative working relationship. One might say that church and state worked hand in hand in a ritualized form of sympathetic magic.

Shamans, when professionally engaged, contrived to look as much as possible like the spirit powers whose protégés they were. Long, uncut, and generally undressed hair was the crowning glory of the shaman. Bear or sealskin robes trimmed with ermine and mink were worn by affluent shamans in cold weather; deerskins clothed others of less wealth. Masks were the most important possessions of the shaman, but carved wood boxes also contained an intriguing assortment of rattles, clubs, soul-catching devices, and knives made of bone, stone, or hammered raw copper. Sacred words and secret songs imparted to him in visions and trances were also guarded personal possessions. When retained to minister to an afflicted person, the doctor-shaman generally would dance, chant, and achieve a state of psychic excitement under the direction of his spirits. (Attributes of these diverse spirits are detailed in the captions explaining the masks illustrated.)

In coastal British Columbia and around Puget Sound in Washington, several shamans might be called to retrieve a soul from "the house of the cannibal spirit" or some other remote and mysterious place where spirits were holding the lost soul because of the breaking of a taboo or some other offense. Souls were often snatched away by spirits who were cooperating with an enemy of the stricken person—not evil spirits, as previously noted, but spirits under the control of a powerful person who was himself evil. Such witchcraft, when discovered, was punished by death or public disgrace and shame when the misdeed was obvious. A team of shamans, when retained for such a mission, often lined up and, while chanting, appeared to paddle an imaginary canoe to the hiding place of the lost soul. At the proper time the head shaman would lapse into a trance, and then his own spirit—or vitality—would leave his body and go to the lost soul, which would be captured and brought back to the spirit canoe. All of the shamans would then "row" the canoe back to the patient, and the head shaman would leap around the room while continuing his chants to the accompaniment of rattles wielded by his assisting shamans. After further inspired and awesome rituals, the head shaman restored the captured soul to the patient's body, which would come to life after its long period of inactivity or listlessness. Shamans seldom claimed to be more than spirit-filled intermediaries between men and the spirit world, but when wearing their masks, they became one with their tutelary spirits, and their effectiveness was assured because the spirits concerned took control. The deeper

226

This Hawk guardian spirit mask once owned by a Kwakiutl at Alert Bay on Vancouver Island represented powers including acutely sharp eyes and hunting skills. Favored as a lineage crest, ownership of such symbols caused frequent warfare between Kwakiutl and Haida chiefs. Collected by D. C. Scott in 1922, black, blue, brown, green, red, and white paint decorated this 10-inch mask. NMC by Joseph H. Wherry

the ecstasy of the shaman—or his trance, as the case might develop—the more effective would be his spirits. Illnesses were treated quite differently (unless caused by soul loss), usually by massaging and sucking on the afflicted portion of the patient's body. Frankly, the foregoing use of the past tense does not tell all of the story, because shamans still practice their arts, albeit quite secretly, along the Northwest Coast.

Down the coast and into California masks were generally unknown except as mentioned, but the healing arts were as mysterious and marvelous, employing visible crystal and bonelike objects which were "the sickness." Unless these were removed by sucking doctors, the patient would waste away and die. This practice still exists in several remote places. One case is said to have been observed by an anthropological research team in a very recent year. When the shamaness sucked out the object of "sickness" and then removed it from her own mouth where she had captured it, the academic investigators requested permission to photograph it. Most agreeably, the shamaness held the object up for a close view, but the camera tripod is said to have collapsed violently without visible cause. Incidentally, the author's informant is a well-educated non-Indian of professional standing, a reputable but baffled witness.

The placating of offending spirits (not necessarily evil, be it noted) as well as the invoking of beneficent spirits was common also in the Plateau and Basin regions. Chief Moses, the great Sinkiuse leader who was also highly respected as the possessor of strong medicine, invoked his Swan spirit to heal the warrior Seven Shirts after he had been gravely wounded in battle with Colonel George Wright's troops during the widespread wars in eastern Washington in the 1850s. Northeast on the plateaus, the Kootenai, Kallispel, and Flathead shamans entered upon their professional careers after publicly telling tribal assemblies of visions and dreams. Mass dances invoking guardian spirits were celebrated in the winter by these tribes and the neighboring Nez Perce. The Kootenai would gather by bands on the shores of the lakes in northern Idaho and eastern Washington for such occasions, and they firmly believed that their dead brothers and sisters would reappear at some vague future time. Though this custom has a messianic—even Christian—flavor, the old ones used to say that these events took place "before anyone ever saw a white man."

Other tribes on the northwestern rim of the Plateau Region, the Lillooet for example, used some masks much like those of the coastal tribes in their winter ceremonies. When a Lillooet tribesman was visited during a dream by a spirit, the entire band celebrated by fasting and bathing in the morning. Afterwards a solemn circle dance was conducted under a shaman's direction. A great feast at high noon followed. The culmination of the spiritual experience was a mass invocation to the Chief of the Dead. The latter deity was regarded similarly by most of the Plateau tribes.

Skilled shamans increased their influence with visions of game herds. The westernmost Shoshoni, the Paiute, and the Snake awaited the inspiration of the shamans' spirits before making preparations for hunts or game roundups when large bands would spread out to drive the antelope and other big game into box canyons or brush corrals. In the Basin, shamans dreamed as elsewhere, and many of them were protégés of the spirit of Buzzard, whose power was particularly effective against the venom of rattlesnakes, which were—and are—abundant in the region. During historic times game of all kinds was sorely lacking in most of the Basin, but prior to 1800 the opposite was the case, with buffalo even being available to the Indians, as the endpaper map indicates. Before the sixteenth century, as a matter of fact, the huge beasts roamed over most of the Far West with the exception of Arizona, southern Nevada, California west of the Sierra, western Washington, and Oregon. As recently as 1830 there were still buffalo as far west as southeastern Idaho and northeastern Utah. Thus the tradition of buffalo

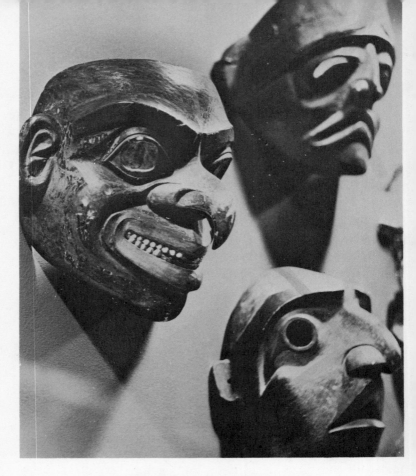

This Tlingit shaman's mask portrays Eagle as a tutelary spirit who assists in curing rituals. It is approximately 9 inches high, with shell teeth, painted blue-green, red, white, and black. AMNH by Joseph H. Wherry

hunting by the ancestors of the Indians of the West and Southwest is well founded and lends historic background to the Buffalo Dance still performed by several of the Pueblo tribes whose ancestors knew the shaggy animals.

The idea of personal spirit helpers was well established among the varied tribes of southern California, where a cult based upon jimsonweed flourished. Called "Jamestown

230

weed" by the first colonists around that Atlantic coastal town, the genus *Datura stramonium* is a large, thorny, bad-smelling plant containing atropine and other alkaloids. Belonging to the nightshade family, jimsonweed, as it is commonly called, is poisonous. However, many Indians over much of the United States and Canadian border regions made tea by boiling the leaves for use as an anesthetic. In southern California this tea was ceremonially drunk by adolescent boys and young men who sought tutelary spirits. Too much of the jimsonweed tea could prove fatal, but in small to moderate amounts it caused trances and hallucinatory effects. Under such influence, the young braves had visions of animal spirits who taught them prayers, songs, and rituals, enabling them to become great hunters, warriors, and even shamans.

Eating live coals and handling fire without physical harm is said to have been another accomplishment of some of the southwesternmost Shoshonian and Mojave-Yuman peoples. Even today some Indians claim the ability to eat fire. Indeed the use of jimsonweed tea was reported among some of the Pueblo peoples, but on a smaller scale. *Datura* grew wild then as it does now over much of the United States. Tobacco

A Tlingit shaman's mask from the Sitka area. Human hair, green pigment, and extensive use of hammered copper distinguish this ritual mask. USNM by Joseph H. Wherry

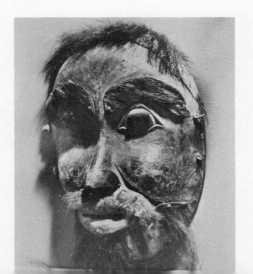

231

Unsual in that it is carved from a whale vertebra, this Tlingit mask was found in a grave house at Cross Sound in southeast Alaska. As a guardian spirit, Raven makes his protégé a skilled hunter. AMNH by Joseph H. Wherry

of several wild species was of greater importance, however, in all of our subject regions. The smoke was usually blown to the four cardinal directions and to the zenith and the nadir in invocation to the spirits and deities at clan and tribal councils or preceding shamanistic healing sessions. In the Southwest tobacco leaves also were rolled inside of corn husks in reasonable counterparts of modern cigars. Some versions of the myth of the adventures of the Navajo Twin Warrior Gods

tell of the preparation of "cigarettes" for the dances conclud-
ing successful ventures against the Enemy Gods or monsters.

In Navajoland religious devotions were—and are—closely
intertwined with healing or blessing ceremonies, which are
essentially of an exorcistic nature, as previously mentioned.
Because of this, medicine men are sometimes suspected of
causing illness by witchcraft in order to collect a fee for healing. Most Navajo will say, however, that the majority of
medicine men are sincere. For "sings" or "chants," the medicine man-priest first prepares a sand painting with stylized
figures representing Turquoise Woman, Talking God,
White Corn Boy and Yellow Corn Girl, and others of the
Holy People with rainbows, hail, lightning, the Four Directions, and other sacred beings. Pollen, powdered corn meal,
colored sand, and various other materials are delicately sifted
to the swept ground by the thumb and forefinger to make
elaborate designs that illustrate the sacred myths. Theoreti-
cally the blues represent turquoise, but the resulting hues are
bluish-gray. (The simpler ground paintings made by the
lower Colorado River tribes are probably the outcome of con-
tacts with the more formalized Navajo.) In a way, the sand
paintings are altars, some of which must be destroyed by
sundown, while others are occasionally used throughout
night-long curing rituals, which must be held in a specially
consecrated hogan or tent that has never been defiled by human habitation.

Four categories of sings are still held despite efforts on the
part of whites to discourage the ancient practice.

Night Chants are complicated ceremonies which attract
"the people" to the site from a wide area. These are a series of
prayers to the Yei-be-chai—the ancient gods, the Holy People
—which last nine days. The many sand paintings, as in the
other chants, illustrate the great myths retold by the singer as
he chants. Very costly, the Night Chants are held to be a re-

newing or revivalistic spiritual experience for all who participate under the leadership of a priest and several assistant
singers.

Fire Chants, sometimes called Mountain Chants, also elaborate and costly ceremonies, take place in the late autumn or
winter to invoke the blessings of the "yei." The Fire Dance
features naked dancers who lash each other with burning
brands while they dance around a fire to the accompaniment
of singing and drumming; this has a purifying purpose.
Feather Dances and other rituals also take place, with pollen
used for face-painting and other rites.

Witch- or Enemy-Spirit-Chasing Chants—sometimes now
called Devil-Chasing Chants—are less expensive, generally
two-day affairs which are held to protect a person, a family,
or belongings from evil or a herd of sheep from depredations,
or for almost any purpose including the curing of sickness.

War Dance or Squaw Dance ceremonies are held during
the summer or early autumn and can be witnessed by visitors.
The primary purpose is to drive out the sickness spirits from
an afflicted Navajo, but there are also social or community
benefits, as indeed there are in all of the Sings. Because this
ceremony permits the mixing of young people of opposite
sexes, romances develop and courting often commences at
such a gathering, where all members of each family concerned have the opportunity to look over the prospective in-
laws. Social dancing in the round and lively feasting on the
meat provided from the sheep or cattle herd of the one who

*A Haida shaman wore this gruesome head-
dress during initiation into the secret shamans' society. The leather torso fitted over
the shaman's head, and the figure's limbs
flapped wildly as the initiate danced while
the "dead man" spirit was invoked. Human
hair topped the 46-inch figure, collected by
James G. Swan prior to 1895. USNM by
Joseph H. Wherry*

"has the Sing" follow the healing rituals. This is the one ceremonial gathering when Navajo maidens are encouraged to capture a likely male and force him to dance until the young man buys his freedom—for the moment at least—with money or other valuable "hard goods" like turquoise or silver jewelry. When the social dancing ends at dawn, a party of mounted warriors attacks the hogan where the curing ritual has been held, and a lively mock battle occurs. The defenders of the ceremonial hogan always triumph with loud war cries when gifts are thrown out the doorway of the hogan with a great show of defiance.

Other sings such as Blessing Way, Hail Chant, Enemy Way, Flint Way, and the like invoke the blessings of nature spirits for physical and mental healing and the overall well-being of an individual or his family. Elaborate costumes and headdresses are worn, but masks among the Navajo are confined to those used in the healing Night Chants of the Yei-be-chai. These masks are sacred and are seldom seen by non-Navajo.

Apache religious ceremonies are related to those of their linguistic relatives the Navajo, but are less elaborate except for the girls' puberty ceremony. Lasting several days and expensive in feast foods, gifts for guests, and fees for the medicine man, the visit of Changing Woman who becomes one with the matured maiden as White Painted Woman is held only rarely in these days. Several years ago the motion picture *Broken Arrow* featured a portion of this magnificent time of feasting and ceremonial tribute to young Chiricahua womanhood.

Apache medicine men are sometimes feared because the supernatural powers are believed to be completely under their personal control. This is particularly so with respect to the Thunder People, supernatural hunters armed with lightning arrows who cause diverse diseases of the mind and body. A

236

Masked and carrying a club carved like a whale, a Chilkat-Tlingit dancer portraying a mythical cannibal giant rushes onstage to attack tribesmen in a dramatic production in the Indian Community House at Haines-Port Chilkoot in Alaska. Many such events are open to the public, as the Tlingit are now reviving interest in their culture.
Alaska State Travel Division

medicine man who employs these spirits to cause harm can be considered an abominable worker of witchcraft who must be discerned by a medicine man with greater power. Having few masks, those which are used represent the Gans—Mountain Spirits—and are employed by the Mescalero in dances which invoke the blessings of these spirits whose abode is in

237

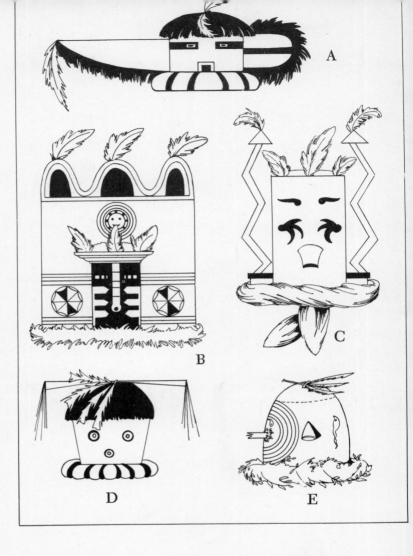

Some of the most important masks of Zuni represent the following deities: (A) Sáyatäsha, who has a turquoise blue face and a single horn; (B) Hémishikwe with cloud symbols at top; (C) Úwanami, one of a number of rain, lightning, and fertility gods; (D) Yámuhakto, with rolled-hide collar at the base of the mask and hair of feathered (probably roadrunner) prayer sticks; (E) Shwani, one of the six Cloud People of the six directions (the priest of Rain and the North, who wears this mask, prays to Awonawilona, the supreme deity who is the cause of all things and synonomous with Sun Father). From *Decorative Art of the Southwest Indians* by Dorothy Smith Sides (Dover Publications, Inc., 1962, courtesy of the publisher)

the mountains. Often erroneously reported as devils or de-mons, the Gans are beneficent nature spirits who bring rain, health, and the good things of life when they are invoked. According to tradition, two old and crippled men had to be left in a mountain cave when their tribe was forced to move away from their village during a war. They were found by six *cahende* who rescued and restored them to health and then helped them find their way to their relatives, who gave thanks for the miraculous deliverance. These are the Moun-tain Spirits, the supernatural benefactors.

In the lands of the Pueblo Indians the religious emphasis is directed toward more than two hundred deities and spirits, some of them ancestral in nature. All live in the underworld from which the Hopi, Zuni, and Keres people came after the creation, and all or most of them return periodically to the world of the living to bestow rain, fertility, and prosperity upon their devotees. Extremely complicated, the religious so-cieties are presided over by a hierarchy of priests and *ca-ciques* (chiefs) who traditionally have equally responsible civil or governing duties. To add further complication, each Pueblo tribal group—and often each village within a tribe—has several distinct religious groups, each with its own priesthood. In general, clan relationships determine the reli-gious affiliations of the clan members. Among the Hopi, for example, the Honau, or Bear clan, enjoys the highest status because this clan's ancestors were the first to emerge from the primal underworld. When the other clans—the Kachina, Angwusi (Raven), Tawamana (Black Bird), Suhubi (Cot-tonwood), etc.—emerged, they were assigned places to live by the people of the Bear clan. Compounding the religious complexity is the grouping of the clans into phratries, of which there are twelve. The clans mentioned above are all in the Kachina (also rendered Katcina) or Sacred Dancer phratry, including the Kachina clan. Another phratry is the

Honani, which also contains a distinct Kachina or Sacred Dancer clan. Other phratries are the Horn Flute, Snake, Water House, Reed, Wood, Cottontail (Rabbit), Earth, Mustard, and Tobacco phratries; each has a number of clans.

The matrilineal organization of society requires the priest-hood to be handed down through the female line. Thus, when a likely lad evidences an interest in the religious traditions of his clan, he may become the protégé of a priestly uncle on his mother's side of his family. Much the same system prevails among all of the Pueblo people. The Kachina clans and the phratry of the same name are not to be confused with the *kachinas* who are the supernatural beings portrayed by the Hopi masked dancers. During the historic period the literally

Buckskin is the basic material of most Pueblo masks. In prehistoric times up until a few generations ago bison hide also was used. These Zuni kachina dolls represent that tribe's clown deities, the Koyemshi, also called Mud-Heads because the round (male) masks are plastered with adobe symbolizing the emergence. The Koyemshi perform amusing stunts, walk on their hands, talk and sing backwards, perpetrate satire during lulls in serious ceremonies, and discipline children. They also carry seeds in the lumps on their primal, form-less heads. The Keresan pueblos call their clown society Koshari. RLMA by Joseph H. Wherry

240

A Keresan tribesman from the pueblo of Laguna performs the magnificent Eagle Dance. Laguna Indians have achieved fame as daring fire fighters throughout the West, where they are employed by the U. S. Forest Service. In "the old days" real eagle feathers were used—some still are. Eagle, after being stopped from growing to monster size, flies so high that he has spirit contact with the sky deities. Therefore, Eagle is an intermediary between medicine men, priests, and the gods. Young men portray the eagle's soaring flight in a dance that actually is a prayer that there will always be many eagles because their feathers clothe the gods. Flagstaff Chamber of Commerce

dozens of Pueblo religious groupings have come to be called kachina cults, and the most practicable way to think of them is as distinct denominations within one theological faith in the same manner as we consider Methodists, Baptists, etc., within the Christian community. As such, the *kachina* societies are not strictly cults because they all combine to give reality to the Pueblo religion as a whole.

The sacred meeting place of a religious society is its *kiva*, a round or square adobe ceremonial hall partially underground with an entryway in the middle of the flat roof. The

241

latter symbolizes the place of emergence to the surface of the earth. All masks and other sacred objects are kept stored in the kiva, which is usually restricted to the men of the society concerned, although there are exceptions to this rule. Long before a ceremony, designated society members prepare the masks or make new ones, make the feather-tipped prayer sticks, arrange the secret altars, and select the dancers who will participate. The *Koshare*, the clowns in Puebloland, mimic the dancers, amuse the crowd during intervals in the ceremonies, and discipline the children. Other participants have made the *kachina* dolls, and they are distributed to the children, who are taught to respect the spirits in whose likenesses the dolls are made. The masks are sacred, and while they are worn the actual spirits of the gods inhabit the dancers. Such spirit possession is transitory and ends when the mask is removed. Prayers are directed to well over two hundred separate spirits and deities, all of whom are beneficent and desirous of blessing the living Pueblo people, who are the descendants of the spirits being invoked.

Best known of the Pueblo religious societies are the rainmakers of Hopi and Zuni and the associated Snake and Bow societies, each of which has an active priesthood. The snakes —live rattlers for the most part—are turned loose after the ceremonies to act as messengers to the gods, who, if pleased with the devotions and rituals, will answer beneficently with rain, which will assure the fertility of the soil and prosperity to the tribe as a whole. This brief summary supplements the comments in preceding chapters. Readers intent upon studying these nature-oriented Pueblo doctrines in depth should consult the definitive works of Walter Collins O'Kane, Ruth L. Bunzel, J. W. Fewkes, Elsie C. Parsons, Gladys A. Reichard, Hamilton A. Tyler, and Ruth M. Underhill, which are listed in the bibliography.

A'cuwa

A'cuwa

K'o'tcininak'o

Gaiyactactaiya

Ko'haiya

Sai'yatac

The deities represented in the ceremonial dances are called katsina by the Keresan peoples. In the mythical age the katsina came to the pueblos in person, but something happened and the people were instructed to make masks and impersonate the deities, who promised to come in spirit. As in other pueblos, the katsina bring rain and promote general health and prosperity. The above are masks of the Keresan pueblo of Sia's katsina-gomaiyawic society:

A'cuwa cróyati (left, top row) is a blue boy's mask with a sunflower symbol on the forehead, a horsehair-and-eagle-feather beard, a bunch of parrot feathers on his head with a parrot, an eagle, and a roadrunner tail feather. This dancer carries the leather strap to which are attached two eagle wing feathers and many eagle neck feathers; a piece of abalone shell dangles from the end.

A'cuwa mékatc (right, top row) is a blue man's mask with beard of red-dyed yucca fiber and a single roadrunner feather on top with bunch of parrot feathers. The A'cuwa appear in a line of a dozen or more dancers.

Kotcinimako are female katsina dancers who appear in groups of four or six; representing the Yellow Women of the North, their masks are yellow. Similar but not illustrated are the Merinako, the Blue Women of the West; their masks are a turquoise color. The Kotcinimako kneel

before the line of A'cuwa dancers and accompany the songs of the latter by rubbing a notched stick with a deerbone while the Merinako dance with baskets in their right hands and spruce twigs in their left. These are the only female dance masks.

Gaiyactactaiya appear in a group of nine (with three Kotcinimako). The faces are turquoise color with white lines over each, red-dyed wool on the forehead, red ears, a collar of fir twigs, and a topnotch of parrot and eagle tail feathers.

Ko'haiya represents Bear; nine dancers. The face is blue-green with cotton on top of mask and a red-headed, yellow-and-red-striped snake on each side of head (reminiscent of the small, poisonous coral snakes). The nose is bright yellow. Low on back of the head is a bunch of owl feathers. The collar is wildcat fur, and four long eagle tail feathers are at the back of the head.

Sai'yatac is present in two masks, representation not known. Somewhat forbidding, this deity could refer to buffalo: the horns are turquoise color; red goat wool and eagle feathers top the head; and the black face has a red triangle above the eyes, bearskin below the mouth, and a wide wildcat collar. These dancers are stern and flail yucca whips wildly as they dance. From Bureau of American Ethnology Bulletin 184 by Leslie A. White, 1962

The Masks

In the Arctic North the masks are among the most delicately crafted to be found anywhere. Carved and painted wood face pieces are fitted with slender, outward-radiating whale baleen. Feathers and small carvings representing animal spirits—*tornait*—are attached to the latter. An additional carving of a seal, a fox, or another animal may be fastened along one side of the mask face piece. Red, black, and occasionally blue are the predominant colors of Eskimo masks. Animal fats are mixed with charcoal, berry juices, and the like to make pigments. Large unpainted areas are common on Eskimo masks, and miniatures are worn on the fingers of women dancers.

The Indians of the Northwest Coast shared with their Eskimo neighbors the belief that all animals, fish, and birds possessed a dual form. The nucleus of their human form, the *inua*, or inner spirit, was somewhat synonomous with thinking and the soul. Whenever the creature decided to show its *inua*, it simply raised its face, beak, or wing or parted its breast feathers in the case of birds to reveal the inner spirit as did Thunderbird in the Kwakiutl myth related in Chapter Two. If the creature wished to assume human form, it shed its feathers or fur coat, and the transformation was instantaneous. Such beliefs led to the development of ingenious double and triple masks with movable beaks and faces which opened outward in halves.

The Kwakiutl of Vancouver Island were the most skilled makers of such complex masks. Carvers all along the Northwest Coast were well paid in dentalium, sable, and other rich furs and fine canoes for their skills. Thus some carvers rose to highly respected positions in the caste-conscious society. Often the mask carvers worked on totem poles, which in-

Go'maiowic

Nye'nye'k'a

Kaci'na

Ctiwictiwa

Tsatcra'ti

Dya'nyi

More Masks of the Gomaiyawic Society from Sia:

Gomaiyawic have clown duties like the Koyemshi or "mud-heads" of the Zuni. Represented by four dancers, the masks are of soft deerskin and the lumps contain seeds; spruce twigs surround the seed lumps; the face is oxide-red like the soil, with a white nose; the collar is black wool.

Nye'nye'k'a, worn by one dancer, has a black face with white designs and protruding eyes; the collar is wildcat fur, and a skunk tail hangs from the topnotch. This spirit carries a yucca-leaf whip in his right hand, a bow and arrow in his left. He is stern and menacing.

Kaci'na, a distinct spirit, is not to be confused with the Katsina group as a whole. Brilliant with a blue-green face, red tablike ears, and a black nose, the head is topped by blue-green tablita with a triple white-cloud design and zigzags representing lightning; at the sides are eagle and parrot tail feathers.

Ctiwictiwa is represented by one masked dancer who portrays the kildeer, a bird related to plovers. The face is yellow with a black, a white, and a red circle, the inside of which is blue-green with white eyes and nose. The tablita on top of the head is blue and yellow and has eagle feathers; the ears are red; the collar is spruce twigs. This spirit dances with eagle feather and bowl of corn in his left hand and a gourd

rattle in his right. His duty is to prepare a "road" for the other dancers.

Tsatcra'ti is "someone with horns" and is represented by two dancers. The face is black with bulging eyes and a bright green triangle on the forehead. The blue-green horns have red tips; the head is topped with wool and an eagle feather and has a black bearskin chin. A grim deity, he carries a whip in each hand.

Dya'nyi is from the Kwiraina Society. Fourteen dancers in a line represent deer and wear real deer antlers and ears on top of the masks; the ears are dyed green outside, red inside. The blue-green face has yellow-and-red-striped snakes on each side of the green eyes and bulging nose, the latter tipped with black. The collar is of spruce twigs. Above the red band at the top of the face are white scallops symbolizing clouds containing rain.

Most male katsina dancers have nude bodies, often painted with diverse symbolic designs, and wear a kilt of homespun cotton. Most wear a foxskin hanging down from the back of the kilt. A string of shell ornaments with an attached ear of corn is slung over the right shoulder. Leather bands dyed blue or green and spruce twigs are worn on the upper arms, and dyed tufts of cotton are worn below the knees. Skunk-fur-trimmed moccasins, gourd rattles, and prayer sticks are carried by most dancers. From Bureau of American Ethnology Bulletin 184 by Leslie A. White, 1962

creased their wealth. Important chiefs frequently sent messengers considerable distances to obtain the services of carvers and this diffused the stylization of the supernatural and guardian spirit symbols over the entire Northwest Coast region. In addition to wood, materials included abalone shell, animal teeth, bird beaks, shredded cedar bark, fur, and occasionally bits of hammered raw copper. Some bird masks had beaks in excess of six feet long. A few Coast Salish masks must have been traded to their linguistic kin east of the Cascade range, because some of the northern Plateau region Salish are known to have used similar masks in their winter ceremonies.

The winter dances were the occasion for dramatic productions of near-epic proportions among the Kwakiutl, Coast Salish, Bella Coola, and Nootka, and the Haida, Tlingit, and Tsimsyan of the northern half of the region. The great, rough-hewn, red-cedar-plank dwellings of these vigorous maritime tribes housed extended families, with as many as fifty or more persons living under the same roof. Each nuclear family had its own private apartment and fire located along the sides of the house. The lower the rank in the extended family, the closer was the living space of that person or group to the doorway, which was usually an opening through the base of a totem pole which graced the front of the house.

The house, village, or clan chief lived at the rear end of the house in a spacious apartment which extended the full width of the building. In front of the painted boards hiding the chief's sanctuary was a grade, a full-width raised floor of planks. Serving as stages, such platforms were the scenes of splendid dramas portraying the regional myths and episodes in the life of the great chief. All of the actors were costumed and masked. Occasionally there were trap doors in the stages through which new supernatural representations appeared or

246

A group of Keresan masks from Sia pueblo from several of the many Katsina societies:

Ckacac, sometimes called Na'wic, is a very small mask worn by a young boy who must be reliable and worthy of the Katsina secrets. It is black with white dots, red ears, and a large red circle in center of face, inside of which the color is blue-green. Spruce twigs, a bunch of owl feathers, and two large turkey wings top the mask; the collar is also of spruce. This mask is owned by the Fire Society.

Ocatc, another Fire Society mask, is worn by two dancers and is shaped of soft deerhide dyed blue-green with flowers painted on the forehead. The chin is black fur (most likely bear), the collar is wildcat skin with fur attached, the horns are red, and the magnificent eagle feathers are natural.

Mai'Dyana is of the Giant Society and is impersonated by seven dancers. The yellow face has black-stepped (cloud) lines at each side of a vertical black stripe containing white circles. The collar is spruce twigs; the ears are red. On top of the mask is a tablita of blue-green with a red band topped by four white rain clouds. In middle of the tablita is one vertical parrot tail feather flanked by two eagle tail feathers.

Go'o'K'iwa, also from the Giant Society, has a blue-green face with red mouth, eyes, nose, eyebrows, and ears. The mask is topped with raw cotton, four eagle wing feathers, and two shoots of wild grass. Beneath the mouth are a hair beard and a wildcat fur collar. Two Go'o'K'iwa enter the plaza tied together. Released by the Koshairi, they rush about lashing the uninitiated with their yucca whips and disciplining children to make them pay attention to the ceremonies.

Si'k'iri, a Giant Society mask, worn by two dancers, has a black face, green nose and eyes, and red ears. Four eagle tail feathers on top of unspun cotton are crossed by a red-tipped arrow which has eagle down fastened to the shaft. The beard is of hair; the collar is a wildcat pelt.

No'wira is worn by one Snake Society dancer. He represents a very old Katsina hotcanyi, or chief, and is escorted to the ceremonial location in the pueblo plaza by the chief of the Snake Society. Carrying a bow and arrow in his left hand and a long flint knife in his right, his horned animal mask is black with a green crescent to the rear of each protruding eye. The mouth is red with white teeth, and a tuft of red wool dangles from the base of each horn. At the back of the mask are owl body and eagle tail feathers; the collar is cut from a wildcat skin. From *Bureau of American Ethnology Bulletin 184* by **Leslie A. White, 1962**

Hopi means "happy and peaceful," and to this could be appended "humble," a characteristic of this tribe, which is related linguistically to the more numerous Shoshonean tribes. In their kivas the religious and curing societies have time for quiet contemplation. This is a portion of an old altar panel showing White Chin, an ancient kachina (possibly female) who was last impersonated in 1895. The round symbols seem to be a variant of those used to signify the sunflower. RLMA by Joseph H. Wherry

disappeared miraculously. Aiding such prestigious dramatic effects were assistants who, on cue, would divert the attention of guests by pouring animal oils on the fire. When the flames leaped high, new characters appeared on stage as if by magic. Voices sounded as if they came from out of nowhere by means of speaking tubes made of lengths of hollow kelp. A few winter ceremonies still occur, and there is a revival of interest in preserving the ancient traditions, particularly among the Chilkat-Tlingit people associated with Alaska Indian Arts at Port Chilkoot, where mask carving is enjoying a renaissance. Among the Nootka and Kwakiutl of Vancouver Island and the tribes around Puget Sound, outdoor dramas were popular when the spirits controlling the elements permitted.

In California the few masks which are said to have hidden the faces of the Kuksu dancers in ages past have not been displayed publicly since the coming of the camera, according to informants. Happily, however, masks are carefully preserved in the Southwest region by the Navajo, whose rare Yei-be-chai masks are the only ones used ceremonially. Most au-

The Hopi Butterfly Dance commemorates the growth of everything that lives and is performed only by the Butterfly clan, who came to Hopi from the pueblos on the Rio Grande before Europeans invaded their lands. The male dancer is painted with the line of life the length of his body, and he wears bells below his knees. At each side maidens hold evergreen branches and wear black mantas beneath colorful outer capes. The tablita headdresses have stepped designs symbolizing clouds and are brilliantly painted with corn and sunflower symbols. On top are feathered prayer sticks. Flagstaff Chamber of Commerce

thorities agree that the Navajo acquired their mask-making skills from the Pueblo peoples and this contention is born out by the masks' similarities. The Apache too have masks; those representing the Mountain Spirits have been mentioned.

Among the Pueblo tribes most masks are rather small and highly stylized. There are some exceptions, though, like the magnificent eagle forehead masks and dancing costumes of Laguna. Exceptionally conservative and understandably wary of visitors, the Pueblo tribes guard their masks jealously and use them only for religious occasions, when they are more often seen than photographed. There, too, the mask maker commands respect for his knowledge of the ancient traditions and skill with deerskin and feathers. Pueblo masks with round heads usually portray male supernaturals, while square masks depict female beings. This is not a fixed rule, however, and round masks can portray high deities while the square ones represent lesser spirits.

Basically the Pueblo masks are made of hides, while gourds or carved wood are used for beaks, ears, etc. Feathers, particularly eagle-down and breast feathers, are used for mask crowns. The paint colors can span the spectrum, and cloth, herbs, bark, and fir sprigs are used for trim.

Southwest customs prescribe more reverence with respect to masks than obtains on the Northwest Coast. The Hopi, for instance, use only the left hand when putting on or removing the mask, and this tradition is also observed in some of the Keres pueblos. So sacred are the masks in Puebloland that many of them are addressed as *kachinas*, because when worn, they are the abode of the spirits represented. Youngsters who have not yet been initiated into any of the myriad of sacred societies are never permitted to look upon a ceremonial *kachina* dancer with his mask removed, nor can many masks be viewed by children or adults unless they are being worn ceremonially under the direction of a priest.

Exquisitely carved and painted by Frederick Neyron of the Hopi village of Oraibi is this Eagle kachina doll. Eagle kachina dancers of Hopi duplicate this costume, for which a full buckskin mask is used. The Hopi version of this dance is also a prayer.
RLMA by Joseph H. Wherry

Pueblo masks are never carelessly or casually hung on a wall or stored in a box. When not in use or being employed as an altar piece in a kiva, the mask is secluded in a sacred place or shrine under the supervision of a priest. Pollen or sacred corn meal is sprinkled over some of the masks before and after being worn, and many in use today are very old.

If the preponderance of masks made by the Northwest Coast tribes seems out of balance in this volume, it is because the masks in that region were more numerous and more extensively worn. Not only were they worn during shamanistic society meetings and for spirit representations, but they were used also in public dramas, in warfare, and when receiving guests, and were displayed as status symbols. The masks themselves were not always regarded as sacred by that region's natives. Indians of the Southwest would be scandalized at the casual treatment accorded the fantastic masks of the Northwest.

To the Navajo, Apache, and Pueblo tribes—and indeed to the Indians of California and elsewhere with regard to their ceremonial headdresses—these artifacts are as sacred as are the relics and ikons of Christendom, a fact utterly disregarded by the early missionaries who forced the natives to destroy or part with them.

A century and a quarter ago, in *The Adventures of Captain Bonneville*, Washington Irving drew upon Bonneville's personal journals. After living for some time among the Nez Perce and the Flathead tribes before either had become acquainted with the ways of whites, Bonneville recorded his feelings for the people most "Americans" called savage redskins:

Simply to call these people religious would convey but a faint idea of the deep hue of piety and devotion which pervades their whole conduct. Their honesty is immaculate, and their purity of purpose and their observance of the rites of their religion are most uniform and remarkable. They are certainly more like a nation of saints than a horde of savages.

Suggested Related Reading

BASSO, KEITH H., *The Gift of Changing Woman*. Anthropological Paper, No. 76, Bureau of American Ethnology, Bulletin 196, 1966.

BENEDICT, RUTH, *Tales of the Cochiti Indians*, Bureau of American Ethnology, Bulletin 98, 1931.

BOAS, FRANZ, *The Mind of Primitive Man*. New York, The Macmillan Company, 1911.

———, *Kathlamet Texts*. Bureau of American Ethnology, Bulletin 26, 1901.

———, *Primitive Art*. Gloucester, Massachusetts, Peter Smith, 1962.

———, *Tsimshian Texts*. Bureau of American Ethnology, Bulletin 27, 1902.

———, *The Central Eskimo*. Bureau of American Ethnology, 6th Annual Report, 1888.

BOURKE, JOHN G., *The Medicine-Men of the Apache*. Bureau of American Ethnology, 47th Annual Report, 1932.

BROWN, WM. COMPTON, *The Indian Side of the Story*. Washington, Okanogan, 1964.

BUNZEL, RUTH L., *Introduction to Zuni Ceremonialism*. Bureau of American Ethnology, 47th Annual Report, 1932.

CATLIN, GEORGE, *Episodes From "Life Among the Indians" and "Last Rambles,"* Marvin C. Rosse, ed. Norman, Oklahoma, University of Oklahoma Press, 1959.

COLLIER, JOHN, *Indians of the Americas*. New York, W. W. Norton & Company, 1947.

COLTON, HAROLD S. and BAXTER, FRANK C., *Days in the Painted Desert and the San Francisco Mountains*. Museum of Northern Arizona, 1932.

COOLIDGE, MARY ROBERTS, *The Rain-Makers*. Boston, Houghton Mifflin Company, 1929.

DEVEREUX, GEORGE, *Mohave Ethnopsychiatry and Suicide: The Psychiatric Knowledge and the Psychic Disturbances of an Indian Tribe.* Bureau of American Ethnology, Bulletin 175, 1961.

DIXON, R. B., *The Northern Maidu.* Bulletin of the American Museum of Natural History, Vol. XVII, Part III, 1905.

DRIVER, HAROLD E., *The Americas on the Eve of Discovery.* Englewood Cliffs, New Jersey, Prentice-Hall, Inc., 1964.

————, *Indians of North America.* Chicago, University of Chicago Press, 1961.

DRUCKER, PHILIP, *The Northern and Central Nootkan Tribes.* Bureau of American Ethnology, Bulletin 144, 1951.

DUFF, WILSON, *The Upper Stalo Indians of the Fraser Valley, British Columbia.* Memoir No. 1, British Columbia Provincial Museum, 1952.

DURKHEIM, EMILE, *The Elementary Forms of Religious Life*, trans. by Joseph Ward Swain. New York, Collier Books, 1961.

EGGAN, FRED, *Social Organization of the Western Pueblos.* Chicago, University of Chicago Press, 1950.

FEWKES, J. W., *Tusayan Katcinas.* Bureau of American Ethnology, 15th Annual Report, 1897.

FORBES, JACK D., ed., *The Indian in America's Past.* Englewood Cliffs, New Jersey, Prentice-Hall, Inc., 1964.

————, *Warriors of the Colorado.* Norman, Oklahoma, University of Oklahoma Press, 1965.

FORDE, C. DARYLL, *Ethnography of the Yuma Indians.* University of California Publications in American Archaeology and Ethnology, Vol. XXVII, No. 4, 1931.

FRACHTENBERG, LEO J., *Alsea Texts and Myths.* Bureau of American Ethnology, Bulletin 67, 1920.

GIDDINGS, RUTH WARNER, *Yaqui Myths and Legends.* Tucson, University of Arizona Press, 1959.

GIFFORD, E. W., *The Kamia of Imperial Valley.* Bureau of American Ethnology, Bulletin 97, 1931.

GODDARD, PLINY E., *Life and Culture of the Hupa.* University of California Publications in American Archaeology and Ethnology, Vol. I, No. 1, 1903.

HARRINGTON, JOHN P., *Karok Indian Myths.* Bureau of American Ethnology, Bulletin 107, 1932.

HIBBEN, FRANK C., *The Lost Americans.* New York, Thos. Y. Crowell Co., Apollo Edition, 1961.

HILL, W. W., *Navaho Warfare.* New Haven, Yale University Press Publications in Anthropology, No. 5, 1936.

HOFFMAN, WALTER J., *Miscellaneous Ethnographic Observations on*

Suggested Related Reading

Indians Inhabiting Nevada, California, and Arizona. Tenth Annual Report of the Heydon Survey, 1878.

HOUGH, WALTER, *The Moki Snake Dance.* The Santa Fe Railway, 1902.

HUMPHREY, SETH K., *The Indian Dispossessed.* Boston, Little, Brown, and Company, 1906.

ILIFF, FLORA GREGG, *People of the Blue Water.* New York, Harper & Row, 1954.

IRVING, WASHINGTON, *The Adventures of Captain Bonneville.* Philadelphia, 1837, and Binfords & Mort, 1954.

JENNESS, DIAMOND, *The Indians of Canada.* National Museum of Canada, Bulletin 65, Anthropological Series No. 15, 1932.

———, *The Faith of a Coast Salish Indian.* British Columbia Provincial Museum, Memoir No. 3, 1955.

KELLY, ISABEL T., *Southern Paiute Shamanism.* University of California Press, Anthropological Records, Vol. II, No. 4, 1939.

KLUCKOHN, CLYDE, *Navajo Witchcraft.* Boston, Beacon Press, 1962.

KROEBER, A. L., *University of California Publications in American Archaeology and Ethnology.* University of California Press, Vol. 38, 1939.

———, *Handbook of the Indians of California.* Bureau of American Ethnology, Bulletin 78, 1925.

LAFARGE, OLIVER, *As Long as the Grass Shall Grow.* London, Longmans, Green & Co., 1940.

LANCASTER, RICHARD, *Piegan.* New York, Doubleday & Company, 1966.

LÉVY-BRUHL, LUCIEN, *How Natives Think.* New York, Washington Square Press, 1966.

LINDQUIST, G. E. E., *The Indian in American Life.* New York, Friendship Press, 1944.

LIPPS, OSCAR H. *The Navajos.* Cedar Rapids, Iowa, The Torch Press, 1909.

MALLERY, GARRICK, *Picture-writing of the American Indians.* 10th Annual Report, Bureau of American Ethnology, 1893.

MARTIN, PAUL S., QUIMLEY, GEORGE I., and COLLIER, DONALD, *Indians Before Columbus.* Chicago, University of Chicago Press, 1947.

MEAD, MARGARET, *People and Places.* Cleveland, The World Publishing Company, 1959.

MERRIAM, C. HART, *Ethnographic Notes on California Indian Tribes.* Robert F. Heizer, ed. University of California Archaeological Research Facility, Department of Anthropology, 1966.

MOONEY, JAMES, *The Ghost Dance Religion and the Sioux Outbreak of 1890.* Part 2. 4th Annual Report, Bureau of Ethnology, Washington, 1896; abridged edition, with Introduction by Anthony F. C. Wallace, published by the University of Chicago Press, 1964.

Suggested Related Reading

MORGAN, LEWIS H., *Houses and House-Life of the American Aborigines*, Washington, 1881; reissued, with an Introduction by Paul Bohannan, Chicago, University of Chicago Press, 1965.

O'KANE, WALTER COLLINS, *Sun in the Sky*. Norman, Oklahoma, University of Oklahoma Press, 1950.

OPLER, MORRIS EDWARD, *An Apache Life Way*. Chicago, University of Chicago Press, 1941.

PARSONS, ELSIE C., *Pueblo Indian Religion*, two volumes. Chicago, University of Chicago Press, 1939.

RADIN, PAUL, *Primitive Religion, Its Nature and Origin*. New York, Dover Publications, Inc., 1957.

RAY, VERNE F., *Primitive Pragmatists, The Modoc Indians of Northern California*. Seattle, Washington, University of Washington Press, 1963.

REICHARD, GLADYS A., *Prayer: the Compulsive Word*. Locust Valley, New York, J. J. Augustin, 1944.

——, *Navajo Religion*. Princeton, New Jersey, Bollingen Foundation, Inc., and Pantheon Books (2 volumes), 1950.

RUBY, ROBERT H., and BROWN, JOHN A., *Half-Sun on the Columbia, A Biography of Chief Moses*. Norman, Oklahoma, University of Oklahoma Press, 1965.

RUSSELL, FRANK, *The Pima Indians*. Bureau of American Ethnology, 26th Annual Report, 1908.

SCOTT, LALLA, *Karnee, A Paiute Narrative*. Reno, Nevada, University of Nevada Press, 1966.

SETON, ERNEST THOMPSON, and SETON, JULIA M., *The Gospel of the Redman*. Seton Village, 1958.

SLOTKIN, J. S., *The Peyote Religion: A Study in Indian-White Relations*. New York, The Free Press, 1956.

STERN, THEODORE, *The Klamath Tribe*. Seattle, Washington, University of Washington Press, 1965.

STEVENSON, MATILDA C., *The Zuni Indians: The Mythology, Esoteric Societies, and Ceremonies*. Bureau of American Ethnology, 23rd Annual Report, 1904.

STEWARD, JULIAN, *Basin-Plateau Aboriginal Sociopolitical Groups*. Bureau of American Ethnology, Bulletin 120, 1938.

STRONG, EMORY, *Stone Age on the Columbia River*. Portland, Oregon, Binfords & Mort, 1960.

SUTTLES, WAYNE, *Katzie Ethnographic Notes*. Memoir No. 2, British Columbia Provincial Museum, 1955.

SWANTON, JOHN R., *The Indian Tribes of North America*. Bureau of American Ethnology, Bulletin 145, 1953.

——, *Haida Texts and Myths*. Bureau of American Ethnology, Bulletin 29, 1905.

Suggested Related Reading

THOMPSON, LAURA, *Culture in Crisis: A Study of the Hopi Indians*. New York, Harper & Brothers, 1950.

THOMPSON, STITH, *The Folktale*. New York, Holt, Rinehart & Winston, 1946.

TYLER, HAMILTON A., *Pueblo Gods and Myths*. Norman, Oklahoma, University of Oklahoma Press, 1964.

UNDERHILL, RUTH M., *The Navajos*. Norman, Oklahoma, University of Oklahoma Press, 1956.

———, *Red Man's Religion*. Chicago, University of Chicago Press, 1965.

WHERRY, JOSEPH H., *The Totem Pole Indians*. New York, Funk & Wagnalls/Wilfred Funk, 1964.

WHIPPLE, A. W., *Pacific Railroad Report*, Vol. III, Part 3, 1856.

WHITE, LESLIE A., *The Pueblo of Sia, New Mexico*. Bureau of American Ethnology, Bulletin 184, 1962.

———, *The Acoma Indians*. Bureau of American Ethnology, 47th Annual Report, 1932.

WHITING, BEATRICE B., *Paiute Sorcery*. Viking Fund Publications in Anthropology, 1950.

WISSLER, CLARK, *Indians of the United States*. Garden City, New York, Doubleday & Company, Inc., 1953.

WYMAN, LELAND C., *The Windways of the Navaho*. The Taylor Museum, Colorado Springs Fine Arts Center, 1962.

———, *Navaho Diagnosticians*. American Anthropologist, Vol. XXXVIII, 1936.

257

Index of Mythical Beings

Index of Mythical Beings

General Index

Ahtena Indians, 42
Alaska, 5, 6, 36, 42–43, 140, 186
albino
  deer, 175
  redwoods, 178
Aleut, 42, 222
Aleutian Islands, 6, 42
Algonkian linguistic stock, 30
Americans, 32, 35
anesthetic, 231
angakok, 222
  see also medicine men, shamans
animals
  deer, albino, 175
  mythic origin of, 159
ant hill, 12
Apaches de Navajo, 11
Apache Indians, 9, 10–11, 15, 18,
    20, 30, 159, 213, 214
  ceremonies and rituals, 236–239
  masks, 250
  Mescalero dances, 237–239
  myths
    Coyote decreed death, 152
    creation, 213
    Monsters and why Bat has no
      feathers, 126–131;
    Chiricahua version, 131
Arctic Region, 42–43, 180, 218
aristocracy, 40
Arivaipa Indians, 9

Arizona, 9, 11, 17, 18–19, 159
Asia, 5
Athabaskan linguistic stock, 9, 30,
    34, 36, 37–38
Aztec dialects, 12
Aztec-Tanoan linguistic stock, 10,
    11, 15, 23

baleen, 182
balsas, 18, 35
Bannock Indians, 24, 180
Basin Region, 9, 20–26, 159,
    228–229
  clothing, 21
  diet, 20–21, 23
baskets, 15, 24, 30, 39, 42, 75
  feathered, 34
Battle of Wounded Knee, 25–26
beginning, the, 44, 59, 193
Bella Coola Indians, 225
  masks, 246
  myth, Sun Boy and the Cannibal
    Giant, 121–123
  Sun as deity, 186
Bering Sea, 87
Big Head religion, *see* Kuksu
    religion
birds, origin of, 131
"Bird Woman," 23–24
Blackfoot Indians, 131, 136
Blythe, California, 159

263

boat, 43
Bole Maru religion, 200
Bolivia, 35
Bonneville, Captain, 252
bounty hunting, 32
British Columbia, 27, 30, 36, 67,
 114, 124
brush house, 178
buffalo, 25, 29
 range before Europeans came,
 229–230
Bureau of American Ethnology, 32

cactus, 15
California, state of, 9, 20, 23, 29,
 37, 43, 72–73, 114, 177,
 181
California Region, 9, 32–36, 159,
 190, 218, 230–231
 few masks, 249
Canada, 26, 180
Canby, General, 29
candlefish, *see* eulachon
canoes, 29, 34, 36, 39, 43, 70
Cape Flattery, Washington, 140
"Captain Jack," 29
Casa Montezuma, 17
Cascade Mountains, 26, 30, 36,
 95, 124, 131
Catholics, 5
Cayuse Indians, 25, 26
Central Valley, California, 34
ceremonies, 25, 248–249
 annual Fourth of July ceremony
 and feast, 178
 Apache ceremonies and rituals,
 236–239
 burning, 197, 199
 First Salmon, 167–168, 173,
 180
 mourning, 199
 Navajo, 233–236
 Pueblo religious ceremonies,
 239–242
 see also rituals, dances
Chaco Canyon, 12, 159
Changing Woman, 34

Channel Islands, 73
Charbonneau, Toussaint, 24
Chehalis, Washington, 124
Chemehuevi Indians, 23, 24
Chetko Indians, 38, 175
Chicago, 17
Chico, California, 194
Chilcotin Indians, 30
Chilkat tribe, 123
Chimariko Indians' myth, How
 Death Began, 146–150
Chinook Indians, 27, 36–37, 99
 myth, Mentonee and the
 Mountain Spirits, 99–101
 trade with Plateau tribes, 37
Chiracahua tribe, 9, 126
Christian era, 11
 early saints, 225
 see also Judeo-Christian ethic
Chumash Indians, 34
church and state, 225
Cibola, Seven Cities of, 11
cigars, 232
clans, 15, 18, 38, 41
 Eagle clans (Tsimsyan, Haida),
 87, 93
 Frog clan (Tsimsyan), 123
 Grizzly Bear clan (Haida), 87,
 93
 origin of Navajo clans, 211
 Pueblo clans, 239–240
 Salmon-Eater clan (Tsimsyan),
 87–93
Cle Elum, Washington, 131
cliff dwelling, 17
clothing, 30, 40
 in myth, 88
Coast Range Mountains, 55
Coast Salish Indians, 36, 59, 225
 masks, 246
 myth, How Indians obtained fire,
 95–99
 see also Salish Indians
Cochise, Chief, 9
Cochiti Indians' myth, Origin of
 the Cochiti, 155–157
Cocopa Indians, 18

General Index

General Index

Idaho, 20, 24, 26, 30
illness
  treatment of, 227–228
  see also shamans, medicine men
insanity, 124–125, 152
inua, see spirit
irrigation, 15
Irving, Washington, 252

Jicarilla tribe, 9, 126
jimsonweed, 230–231
Joseph, Chief, 29
Judeo-Christian ethic, 44, 217
Juneau, Alaska, 123

kachinas, 12, 13
  societies, 241–242
Kalispel Indians, 30, 221–222
  shamans, 228
Kalispel, Montana, 131
Karok Indians, 55, 75, 175, 177
  myth, Coyote makes People,
    55–59
Kashia Reservation, 178
Kato Indians, 191
  Kuksu religion, 190–192
  myth, Kuksu, 193–200
Keams Canyon, 11
kelp, used as speaking tube, 248
Keres Indians, 214
  emergence place, 155
  masks, 250
  see also Pueblo Indians
Keresan dialects, 11
Ketchikan, Alaska, 87
Khotana Indians, 42
killer whale, 187
Kintpuash (Modoc leader), 29
Kiowa-Apache Indians, 10
Kiowa Indians, 179
kivas, 13, 35, 251
  described, 241–242
Klamath Indians, 29
  myth, Land of the Dead, 154
Klickitat Indians, 29
Kootenai Indians, 30

myth, Giant Beaver makes a
  river, 131–133
shamans, 228–229
Kuksu religion, 190–192
  see also Kuksu myth, 193–200
Kwakiutl Indians, 36, 123, 225
  masks, 244
  myths
    Cannibal Giants, 114–121
    Thunderbird creates and
      teaches, 60–65
  outdoor dramas, 249
  serpents in myths, 140

labret, 71
Laguna Indians' masks, 250
Lakes
  Chelan, 133–135
  Flathead, 131–133
  Mead, 17
  Osoyoos, 133
  Pyramid, 26
  Salt, 23
  Tahoe, 20
  Tule, 29
  Wallowa, 136–137
Las Casas, Bartolomé de, 5
leather trousers, 89
legend, defined, 8
Lemhi Indians, 24
Lewis & Clark Expedition, 23–24
Lillooet Indians, 30, 229
Lipan Indians, 9, 10
Loch Ness, Scotland, 133

magic, 225
  see also shamans, medicine men
Magnuson, Senator Warren G., 6
Maidu Indians, 34, 191
  Kuksu religion, 190–192
  myth, Kuksu, 193–200
maize, 13
Makah tribe, 140
Manson, Washington, 135
Maricopa Indians, 18
Marin County, California, 34

267